THE VOICE OF
PARANOIA

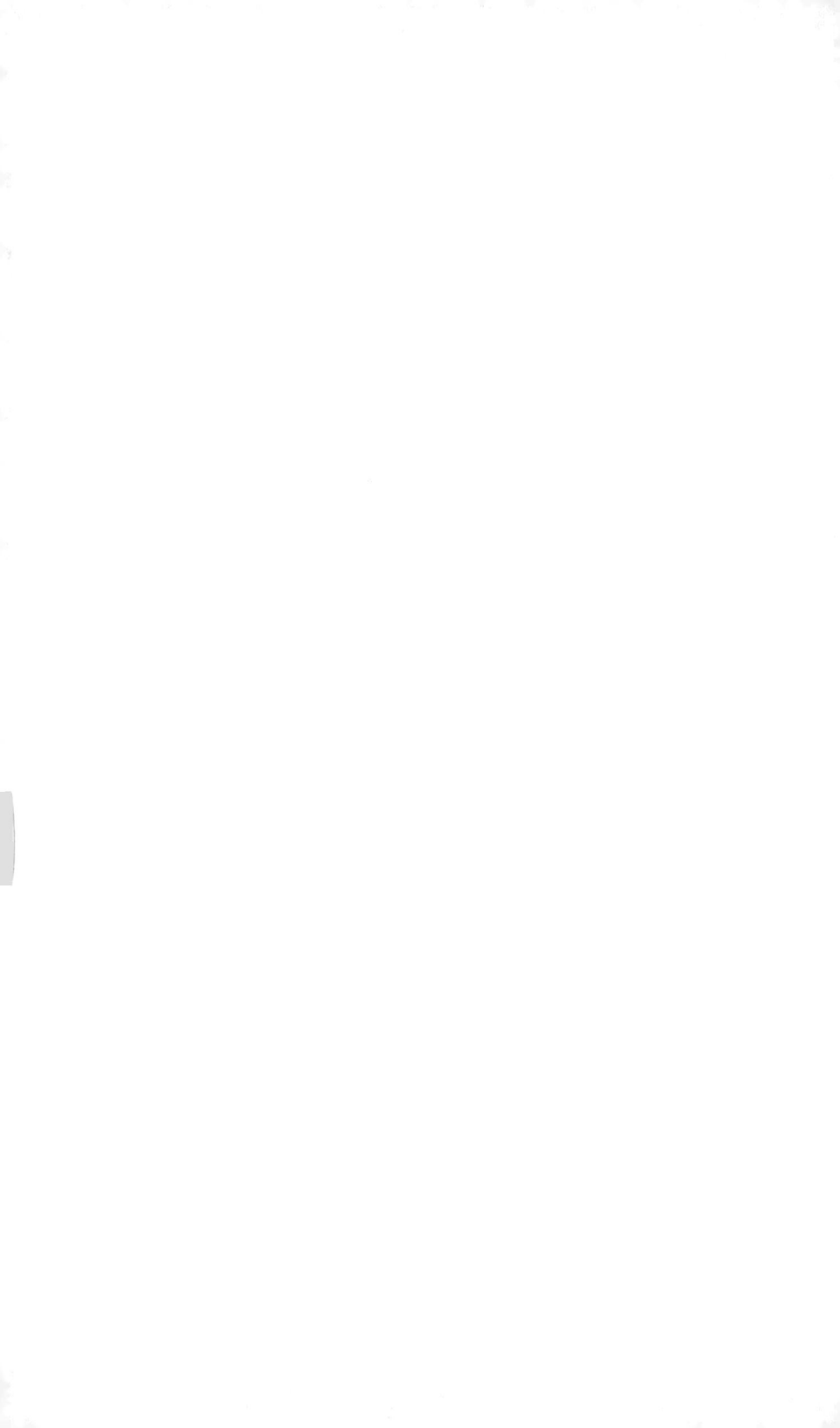

THE VOICE OF
PARANOIA

FROM MISERY TO GREATER AUTONOMY

DANIEL C. MINK

For more information, email dmink.lpc@gmail.com.

ISBN: 979-8-88759-405-7 (paperback)
ISBN: 979-8-88759-406-4 (ebook)

Printed in the U.S.A.

To my wife, Debi, I dedicate this book.

CONTENTS

8

10

PREFACE

I AM VERY EXCITED TO present this book on paranoia and what it means to live a paranoid life. Over the years, I wanted to understand how paranoid people live, the underlying meaning of paranoia, and how it manifests in their lives. To me, paranoid people have a strangeness and mystery about them I could not initially fathom:

> *Who is after them?*
> *Why do they believe people are talking about them and*
>   *saying such negative things?*
> *Why are they so angry and fearful of others?*

When I began researching paranoia, I was disheartened to find few books of depth on the subject. Some old-time writers wrote on various aspects of paranoia, but most books concentrated on suspiciousness and how one might logically deal with suspicions. This seldom proves to be successful. I began my in-depth study of paranoia by going right to the source: paranoid people. I spent 30 years working in a locked hospital ward, youth detention center, and individual clinical practice, and paranoia was often lurking behind many common psychological struggles.

I hope readers gain a deep appreciation for paranoia and how it takes aim at the individual in such negative ways that anger grows and fear increases until they find the help they need. I present a humanistic, phenomenological approach to finding that help. Paranoia is a spectrum of immense distrust that dominates one's life, often unrecognizable at first. I explore *what is* paranoia and *what is not* paranoia. What may start as suspicion may increase to social anxiety, then more intense paranoia as one increasingly avoids healthy interactions with others. Without intervention, paranoia could become a personality disorder.

Many people will recognize themselves here. But be assured, I am not writing about you personally, no matter how much these words find a connection with your life. This book is about the subject of paranoia. I did not intend for anyone's paranoia to lead them to believe that they are the focus of this book. I wrote this mainly for mental health therapists who work with paranoid clients, but social workers, the police force, and other first responders could also benefit since their occupations put them on the front-line pertaining to many paranoid people. With the increased acknowledgment of violence, mental health issues, narcissism, and paranoia in this country, this book can help us understand some of the root causes of social violence.

This book need not be limited to only the professional mental health expert, but deep thinking, paranoid individuals may gain much from its content and possibly motivate them to seek therapy and lower the negative influence paranoia has on them. Mental health experts enjoy reading about psychological phenomena, not only because they meet clients with those issues, but because the phenomena are interesting. Many people deal with paranoia intertwined with other mental health issues, so if this book can arm you with a deeper understanding of paranoia, then I hope it becomes a resource.

I've attempted to remain gender neutral while writing about paranoia. However, based on personal clinical experience, males tend to be paranoid more than females, so I may use the masculine pronoun while referring to paranoid people in general. If I write specifically about a paranoid female, I will use the appropriate female pronoun. I do this not to be biased or sexist, but to aid in the ease of writing.

ACKNOWLEDGMENTS

I MUST ACKNOWLEDGE THE HELP of Dr. Ahmed Faheem and Dr. Safiullah Syed for their input regarding the medical and psychiatric approach to paranoia, including understanding changes in personality and the use of medications to moderate the symptoms of paranoia.

I want to thank my paranoid clients through the many years of practice learning about paranoia, especially the gifted individuals who could describe their paranoia in great detail. That was a blessing. I wish to acknowledge Michael King, Nate Hensley, Pamela Hines-Blue, and Tamara Banks. These fellow Licensed Professional Counselors assisted with reading, editing, and correcting confusing run-on passages and ideas, and making general overall suggestions, graciously contributing their knowledge, expertise, clarity, and time. This book really shaped up after they got their hands on it.

I also wish to thank and acknowledge Jeannie Culbertson, the Noteworthy Mom, for all her help and guidance in bringing clarity to this book. I'd also like to thank, Jude Mag-asin for the cover design, promotion, and success. The illustrations within are the creative drawing of Cheryl Campbell, a most talented graphic designer. Many thanks.

Duquesne University in Pittsburgh, PA, through their Existential/Phenomenological psychology graduate program, guided the development of my deep thinking and philosophical approach to mental illness and human psychology in general.

The greatest gift of an excellent education is that you never have to give it back, only pay it forward.

And finally, my greatest acknowledgment must go to the loving, long-standing, and ongoing support of my wife, Debi. She has kept me honest, motivated, and involved in life. Her keen intuition to identify the root of a problem quickly has helped me dig deeper into my own understanding of paranoia as a lived phenomenon. Her insights have always brought out the best in me.

INTRODUCTION

"WHEN I WAS YOUNG, THERE was a camera hidden in the clock on the living room wall. How else could my parents know everything I was doing? I remember not being able to get away with anything, and everything I did against the rules was punished severely. One day, I took the clock down and inspected it thoroughly but found no camera, only a simple clock doing what a clock does. The next day, the spying clock was back. I was still being watched by the clock and whoever was doing the spying on me. Logic, proof, and common sense could not dissuade my belief. I believed there was no place in the house that I could stand where I was not being observed by someone's eyes.

"From every angle, I believed neighbors could see me and observe every movement and action. I would imagine neighbors using binoculars to see what I was doing in my house when I was alone. I figured they were thinking I was a weird kid, friendless, morally weak, and too scared to play outside with others. They thought I must be hiding something very personal. The only place I felt safe from spying eyes was in the basement. At least there I could relax. I knew only God could see me in the basement, but I believed He judged me harshly as well. I believed there must be something wrong with me if everyone else thought something was wrong with me. I started to distrust people. What earthly reason would a twelve-year-old child think these kinds of thoughts about himself and believed he had to hide? Why were others so interested in me? I had to hide from them and not trust them, whoever they were. I had no one to talk to about all this."

This small glimpse into paranoia is from the life story of Peter in his childhood. (I will refer to Peter often in this book.) He admits he was confused and scared because he did not understand why he thought and felt the way he did. This is remarkably similar to many others' stories I have heard over the years. Let us investigate how one develops paranoia, how it affects one's life, and how one can come to terms with it, easing paranoia's control over one's life.

Most twelve-year-olds are not paranoid, but the seeds of paranoia can germinate early in life. Throughout this book, I will show that paranoia is a psychological problem brought on by lifestyle manifestations that develop and grow in one's life. Paranoia replaced this individual's free, imaginative, inter-co-operative self with an extremely limited, restricted, and rigid worldview. Paranoia is the life lived by a lonely, distrustful individual with low self-esteem. It feeds on itself, developing greater control over the individual unless one consciously takes up the struggle to reduce these restrictions and limitations, learn again to trust others, and genuinely feel positive about oneself.

I wanted to study some aspect of the psychological world that begs further understanding and depth, and my interest has been with this phenomenon—*paranoia*. I wanted to understand the lived-experience of being paranoid. I searched for the essence, the roots, and basic required elements—also called *constituents*—from these people's description of themselves being paranoid. I tried to understand paranoia well enough so that others who are *not* paranoid might better understand the paranoid person's life. This research gave me a clearer, broader, and more inclusive understanding of paranoia, a more precise and understandable meaning that reflects the everyday lived-experience[1] of paranoia. I describe this method more in the first chapter.

Anxiety exists before paranoia became a controlling force in one's life, and remains a central disturbance in the paranoid person's life. Anxiety is as powerful a prerequisite for paranoia as it is for most other emotional and mental problems. No discussion on paranoia can be started without addressing the impact anxiety makes on life. We are born into an anxious and stressful world and struggle with it throughout. One must deal with their paranoia alongside all other mental and emotional disturbances, anxiety being the most powerful and disturbing of these influences. I will discuss anxiety at length as an *a priori* contribution (that which comes before) for paranoia's existence, but I stress that paranoia and anxiety are not equivalent phenomena.

Paranoia is a dysfunction in living, not just another form of anxiety or convoluted thinking. This dysfunction develops until one believes others are:

- out to get them.
- constantly observing them.
- harshly judging them.
- reading their thoughts.

So, what does it actually mean to be paranoid? What is the lived-experience of paranoia in daily interactions with others, oneself, and one's outlook for the future? Although many researchers and writers have speculated on underlying "causes" of paranoia and have tried to explain what has happened in a person's life to make them paranoid, no successful and defini-

---

[1] The compound expression "lived-experience" stands for a unitary phenomenon. It is understood as a whole, an expression of a totality of living prior to any intellectual understanding of information or "causal" events. We are wholly and completely experiencing life in our lived-experience. These types of unitary expressions are used throughout the book.

tive elucidation of paranoia's role or purpose in life has come forth. Not all paranoia has its origins in childhood. As we will see, it can emerge later in life for many reasons. Much research exists on how drug use—especially marijuana and cocaine— can create paranoia in some people; slight symptoms at first, then increasing possession of the personality with the length and intensity of drug use.

Paranoia is understood to be suspicious thoughts one has of being spied upon and watched, and the fear of being "found out" by others who have an uninvited interest in who we are and what we are doing. It is often confused with being anxious and worried. Paranoia is generally believed to manifest suspicions of:

- infidelity.
- being harmed or exploited.
- grudges, anger, and fear.

This current study shows paranoia to be a lifestyle brought on through life circumstances, through the way one lives, and by one's way of thinking about oneself among other people. Paranoia can grow with a person until it becomes a destructive, integral part of their personality.

The constituents of paranoia are its roots, and as in nature, roots feed and nourish growth either in a healthy or unhealthy way, depending on what nutrients are being fed. As our own family roots became our foundation and fed our human tree, we grew and developed through the nurturing we received, along with our individual thoughts, feelings, and decisions. If one has been neglected, abused, and psychologically malnourished, one's roots will find difficulty supporting a psychologically healthy lifestyle, and our human tree may grow in a warped and unhealthy direction.

If we attempt to yank out the unhealthy roots abruptly, we will surely harm our tree's life, and its growth potential and future possibilities could cease. But if we get down there in this soil—psychotherapeutically—do a thorough examination of the roots, look for signs of paranoia, disentangle those roots and provide healthy nourishment, we come to realize how paranoia has negatively and unhealthily fed our growth.

Deep roots have something to teach us. Our human tree now has greater potential to grow in a healthy direction, but what has already been damaged by paranoia may not change. Psychotherapy searches through those psychological roots to help discover what has nourished our mental and emotional lives, the good and the bad. This book begins with examining the roots of paranoia, its impact on one's life, its effects on one's social circle, and how a knowledgeable, experienced therapist can assist with its eradication.

Being one of many possible "phenomena" of human experiences, paranoia stands out as an important psychological structure in the sea of humanity, thrusting one towards defensiveness and imploring one to flee from the crowd. As we begin this investigation into paranoia, we realize there is nothing uncommon about the roots of paranoia–loneliness, distrust, low self-esteem–they are as prevalent in our society as other human experiences such as stress, fear, anger, jealousy, and depression.

Paranoia lives in varying degrees, a spectrum ranging from occasional suspiciousness (social anxiety) to the more extreme forms of schizophrenia. As we begin exploring the structure of paranoia, we will understand why paranoia is fleeting for some, but for others, it may take over their personality. When we break down paranoia into its structural parts, it helps us understand how paranoia is lived by you (if you experience life through paranoid eyes) or by our clients, workmates, friends, or strangers.

Throughout this book, I discuss what it means to the paranoid person to live a lonely existence and how loneliness is an impetus for paranoia. I examine what it means to trust and to distrust, and how this affects the thinking of the paranoid person. Since suspiciousness is a major symptom of the paranoid person's life, I detail the derogatory remarks the paranoid individual "hears" others say about them, why this is of the utmost importance when working with paranoid clients, and how this negatively affects self-esteem.

What is the connection between what the paranoid person "hears" others (seen or unseen) say and his own self-scrutiny? Mentally or physically blocking out the observers is an ineffective way of dealing with paranoia, so I propose a humanistic, individualized approach to assist this person to better understand their paranoia by exploring ways to reduce its control and domination in their life.

The paranoid life is a lonely, distrusting existence, overflowing with low personal self-worth and negative self-judgment. The degrading and judgmental voice of the "other" that the paranoid person hears, informs the therapist what the paranoid person thinks, feels, and believes about themself. It helps the therapist identify what has been preventing them from working toward their life goals. Paranoia can now become the educator, its symptoms teaching a lesson.

In subsequent chapters, I describe methods that clearly examine what paranoia means long-term, how it has taken over a person's life, and how it is an essential life-fulfilling potential for understanding one's need for fulfillment. I discuss how to reduce the isolating and judgmental influences on oneself, and how to build a more integrated life, eventually moving toward healing one's negative self-judgments. It may now be possible for the individual to move away from the strong negative influences of paranoia and develop extensive, durable self-esteem and personality.

During my investigation into paranoia, I came to realize that paranoia acts like an unconscious complex, exerting its effect upon one's consciousness whenever the current lived-situation sparks ebullition. I use the Jungian theory of the *Complex* to work with and better understand paranoia, and I describe how paranoia acts and behaves according to the rules of the complex. The unconscious mind carries the paranoia complex within. When the complex is activated, one is "taken over" by paranoid symptoms, which explains those times when paranoia becomes overwhelmingly dominant in one's life, and accounts for when one seems to be free from or minimally occupied with paranoid symptoms.

Although the paranoia complex may be at rest at times, it is still very much involved in their unconscious life, and when something activates it, it does what complexes do; it explodes emotionally and takes over the rational mind. It inundates this person with paranoid affect, suspicion, and emotion, sending logical thinking and judgment flying out the window.

One of the most essential aspects of working with paranoid clientele is to help them better understand themselves and how they got separated from their "truer" nature. I am speaking of the individuation process at the core of one's psychological purpose and movement through life. By examining one's paranoia and the conscious integration into one's personality, the paranoid client moves along the path of individuation and self-actualization, pushing themself further towards self-understanding. By listening to one's paranoid thoughts, one can identify where one has become blocked along one's individual journey in life. This individuation process is to become who one really is:

> Individuation is an at-one-ment with one-self and at the same time with humanity, since oneself is a part of humanity (Jung, 1954/1966, p. 107).

Ignoring one's paranoia invites a lifetime of lonely and miserable living; plus, there is an increased chance that one's paranoia will grow into a more serious personality disorder. The individual who recognizes their paranoid symptoms and struggles through them benefits from this elucidation and may reduce their paranoia. Common belief from literature is that paranoia is not something one can "get over" or reduce over time, and I agree to some extent, but I have also found that with ongoing conscious integration of the underlying constituents into an increasingly healthy personality, symptoms can decrease.

If one tries to deal with paranoia by oneself in isolation, one tends to fall back into their usual patterns of negative thoughts, beliefs, anger, fear, and suspicious behaviors, thus remaining lost in paranoia. One cannot find one's way out of this darkness alone. Intervention is necessary to help a person overcome paranoia's control over them. It is best to work with a fully competent therapist who understands paranoia and recognizes the necessity of helping their clients work towards the roots that are truly feeding paranoia.

THE ULTIMATE GOALS OF THIS BOOK ARE:

- to understand how paranoia affects a person's entire life.
- to make clear what contributes to paranoia's development and growth, and the paranoid personality.
- to discuss how loneliness, low self-esteem, and distrust negatively influence the paranoid person's life.
- to introduce effective, therapeutic means to working in therapy with individuals who are paranoid.
- to show how paranoia can be a catalyst to assist with the process of individuation.

To the psychotherapist, I would say: paranoid people do not trust you well enough to talk with you—they are much too lonely and isolated to come to your office to see you, too frightened, angry, and self-deprecating to speak up about what really bothers them—but one day, they do show up. So how can you help them?

Paranoia has become a blockade toward their further development. It has impeded their success, comfort, and interpersonal and business relationships. It has degraded them from achieving their highest potential. Understanding paranoia provides us with the opportunity to guide these clients toward hope for a more meaningful and socially interactive life, assist with a reduction of symptoms of paranoia, help reduce the fear and anger of paranoia, and aid with improving low self-image and self-esteem. The therapist can help these clients understand how their current life structure contributes to ongoing paranoia. Therapy helps search for a course of action, a direction toward a better life with themselves and others, hopefully minimizing paranoia's negative impact on their life.

Through the haze of psychological confusion and personality problems, paranoia is a magnifying glass to one's inner beliefs, thoughts, feelings, and actions. Both the therapist and the paranoid individual begin recognizing the inner and outer workings of paranoia with more clarity. Through education and therapeutic work, clients who struggle with paranoia witness a potential "easing" of symptoms and bring about a new relaxed acceptance in relationships, trust, self-esteem, and healthy suspiciousness.

We, as therapists, become the positive stimulus, the outside influence, the catalyst that can help the paranoid person change their life and understand more clearly how paranoia has negatively affected them. Through the insightful therapist's intervention, both client and therapist are propelled further along their own unique path of individuation, and the client moves away from a life of self-contempt, distrust, and loneliness, which is *paranoia*.

THE ROOTS OF PARANOIA

T HE TERM *PARANOIA* IS A construct.[2] It is important to understand a construct through its organizing parts, to know the in-depth essence of its meaning, so as not to get caught up in only words without the important connection to their meaning. Starting with common beliefs and definitions of paranoia, we learn that paranoia is much more than a simple definition. One cannot find the meaning of paranoia in any dictionary, not in an expanded and comprehensive unabridged collegiate dictionary or any massive collection of psychiatric or psychological tomes. The word is certainly found there, but dictionaries cannot convey meaning, only definitions, which we will see differs from the *meaning* of paranoia as people live and experience it. The *Diagnostic and Statistical Manual of Mental Disorders* (5th ed.) describes paranoia as a personality disorder that is:

> A pervasive distrust and suspiciousness of others such that their motives are inter-

---

2   A construct is a fancy word that is used to describe in-depth, observable, or non-observable experiences, cognitive moments or events, and interrelationships between people, objects, and events that help us organize and better communicate about a lived-experience.

preted as malevolent…as indicated by four
(or more) of the following (paraphrased):

- Suspects without sufficient basis that others are exploiting, harming, or deceiving them.
- Is preoccupied with unjustified doubts about the loyalty or trustworthiness of friends or associates.
- Is reluctant to confide in others.
- Reads hidden and demeaning or threatening meanings into benign remarks or events.
- Persistently bears grudges.
- Perceives attacks on their character or reputation.
- Has recurrent suspicion, without justification, regarding fidelity of spouse or sexual partner.

And this does not occur exclusively during
the course of schizophrenia, bipolar disorder, or depressive disorder with psychotic
features (APA, 2013).

The DSM-5 is the common reference for psychiatric diagnoses. But this description lacks depth and substance and states nothing about the intensity of fears, anger, loneliness, distrust, self-esteem, and other contributing factors to paranoia. Another commonly found definition:

"Paranoia is an unfounded or exaggerated
distrust of others, sometimes reaching
delusional proportions. Paranoid individuals constantly suspect the motives of those
around them and believe that certain individuals, or people in general, are 'out to get
them'" (The Free Dictionary, 2021).

This definition is a little closer to the truth of how paranoid people live but still doesn't explain much of the underlying, integral components of the everyday experience of paranoia, i.e., what the paranoid person is actually living through when distrustful and suspicious or who it is that is actually "out to get" them.[3]

> Paranoia is a mental illness that affects all aspects of a person's lived experiences. Van den Berg writes about how mental illness is not a "thing" that a person possesses, but an embodiment of the entire illness. He states, "My intention is to show that a single patient, no matter to which group his illness belongs, embodies the entire psychopathology" (van den Berg, 1972, p. 3).

We do not just have paranoia; we live it and are it—the longer paranoia lives, the more intertwined it becomes in one's personality. We can no more remove someone from their paranoia without affecting their entire life than we can remove one's right leg without affecting their entire way of existing. One's life meshes with one's mental illness. They are enmeshed, fully participating—not necessarily consciously—in their life as a paranoid person, and they cannot find their way out alone.

RESEARCH BASIS

I often discuss paranoia using the metaphor of a stewing pot of soup, its many ingredients being the constituents we find in our phenomenological study of paranoia. Instead of meat, potatoes, and carrots, we find distrust, loneliness, and

---

[3] *Who* is out to get them will prove to be very revealing in the paranoid experience.

low self-esteem flavoring our personality, a bitter taste that becomes suspicious, angry, fearful, and filled with self-doubt and self-ridicule. All the once-flavorful ingredients have slowly changed this person into someone who is now impotent and foul, from a pleasant-tasting mixture to the convoluted and septic taste of paranoia.

I started this research by questioning several people—college students, clients, and others—who believed they were paranoid. All stated they were suspicious of others and did not trust people in general. They did not know why they acted and thought the way they did, but they knew something was not quite right. I asked for a written example of a situation when they believed they were paranoid. I asked them to go into great detail about how this situation started, how they emotionally, physically, and mentally experienced it, what they did during the experience, and how it concluded. I asked them to describe this situation completely and thoroughly so that I could understand what it was like for them.

I continued to collect these kinds of explanations from paranoid people over the years to confirm and verify my findings and expand the results. As I worked with paranoid clients in therapy, I searched for any additional information I could gather to help clarify what the initial research provided. What is the lived-experience—the day-to-day beliefs, thoughts, feelings, emotions, anticipations—of the paranoid person?

PARANOIA: ITS ESSENCE

In this first chapter, we will look at what has been written about paranoia by various theorists and the accepted foundation and understanding of paranoia over the past hundred years or so. Paranoia is just one of a great variety of mental health illnesses that affects humans, and because many people live paranoid lives, we need to know what paranoia truly is.

One's knowledge of paranoia may be based on observation, study, reading, encountering others, or living it. If you, the reader, are not paranoid, you may only know about this kind of experience through books. But for those who live paranoid, or those whose career or family brings them in contact with paranoid people, it is important to understand paranoia to its depth and see the commonality existing in all people paranoid. I don't believe those inadequate definitions of paranoia are sufficient any longer to describe how one lives or sees the world through distorted, paranoid eyes. We are searching for paranoia's *essence*.

All psychological events that humans can experience are called "psychological phenomena." Whether one is talking about being angry, feeling depressed, or being jealous, these and countless others are all phenomena capable of being experienced by human beings. When one examines phenomena closely, one finds that one's experience of a phenomenon is similar to another's experience of that same phenomenon, i.e., humans tend to experience phenomena in similar ways. Our bodies respond to psychological experiences—for example, fear and anger—with similar physiological responses.[4] Regarding the similarity of experiences among all humans as a collective, Van Kaam (1969) states it this way:

> ...experience, with all its phenomena, is basically the same in various subjects. It presupposes that other people experience basically the same sensations, perceptions, images, needs, desires, feelings, and intellectual acts that the scientist experiences.

---

[4] I would refer the reader to the research of Paul Ekman who took facial photographs of various people during intense emotional expression and showed them to people of diverse nationalities, cultures, and age groups, and all agreed on the emotions being portrayed, i.e., the facially expressed emotions were universally recognized.

> This basic identity of experience is an axiom in psychology. The building of experimental psychology rests on this foundation (p. 323).

What makes paranoia so important to understand and study, and what can we learn by studying its depth? Heidegger (1962) defines a phenomenon as "the showing-itself-in-itself" (p. 54). This short but descriptive definition makes the most sense when one is fully conscious of what one is experiencing, not just living an unrealized or blind approach to life's various experiences and moments. We would then understand a phenomenon such as paranoia as "the showing of paranoia as paranoia," but this only makes sense after one has fully investigated paranoia's meaning. Unless we investigate a phenomenon, we may not understand what that experience actually means, even though psychology has given it a name. The actual lived-experience of paranoia is being studied here to emphasize and express the need to spell out and describe completely what that lived-experience means, and to explain that meaning completely. We wish paranoia to show itself for what paranoia is—its essence.

Since paranoia is a human experience, one among abundant experiences, I found it important enough to study and open up its true meaning to increase the general and specific comprehension of what it's like to live a paranoid life. Moreover, through this "revealing" of the meaning of paranoia, it becomes possible to work toward decreasing the unrelenting fear of persecution, suspiciousness, and withdrawal from relationships seen with paranoia. Paranoia is what it is, even if one does not understand it. What is needed is the clarification of the lived-experience, expounding on those insights, finding ways to help those who live a paranoid existence, and assisting them in decreasing their suffering from distrust, loneliness, negative self-judgment, and fear of persecution.

Merleau-Ponty states that we can come to understand our lives and the world because we are cognitive beings who must separate and fully understand what we *think* about a phenomenon from the actual *lived-experience* of that phenomenon. Once a phenomenon has been explored and understood to its very core, to the pure roots of its structure, this is what we call its "essence." He writes:

> The insight into essences rests simply on the fact that in our experience we can distinguish *the fact that* we are living through something from *what it is* we are living through in this fact (Merleau-Ponty, 1964, p. 54).

We can dissect and research paranoia, study it, think about it, question its various constituents, and observe how it manifests in the individual's personal and social life. The researcher separates a phenomenon from the human experience, studies it, sees how it influences human life, and understands it as an essential constituent of life, but does not destroy the integrity of the "whole" human.

PARANOIA OBSERVATIONS

Before we can investigate the true meaning of paranoia and find a comprehensive definition, let us first look at what other researchers have written about paranoia and their understanding of what paranoia is and how it manifests in life. Jung describes paranoia as:

> ...a simple doubling of the personality, which in milder cases is still held together by the identity of the two egos (Jung, 1960, p. 227).

He states that in a person's life, one may develop an antagonistic side to the personality, and if this antagonist side splits from the main ego identity, it becomes an accusatory, demeaning, and derogatory voice of the ego, which then attacks the more sensitive, feeling side of the ego-personality. He continues:

> Obviously at the same time or other the idea of being a persecuted victim gained the upper hand, became autonomous, and formed a second subject which at times completely replaces the healthy ego (Jung, 1960, p. 227).

One's negative personality becomes the accuser. Jung believed that one's intellectual side tries to take over and attempts to destroy all traces of feeling.

In the classic work *The Schreber Case*, Freud described paranoia as repressed homosexual impulses and wishful fantasies. He states:

> We must locate the peculiar character of paranoia…in the particular manifestation of the symptoms, and these we would expect to ascribe not to the complexes but to the mechanism of symptom formation or that of repression. We would say that the paranoid character lies in the fact that the reaction used to fend off a homosexual wishful fantasy is precisely a persecution delusion of this kind (Freud, 1911/2003, p. 50).

In an upcoming chapter, we will examine Freud's belief in the homosexual wish fantasy and attempt to move past this antiquated belief toward a clearer understanding of paranoia.

Sullivan writes about paranoia usually as part of a schizo-phrenic state, but he had much to say about paranoia's origins and roots. Sullivan describes a "me/not-me discord," which is set up between the individual and others. Once a person does not accept the thoughts and negative feelings they have about themselves—such as jealousy, envy, anger, weaknesses, self-revulsion, malice, and inferiority—they dissociate from those thoughts and feelings.

> The beginning of this process comes liter-ally as a sudden insight into some suspi-cion and it comes with a blaze of horror. The suspicion may have hovered around before the sudden insight, and may have been marked by a little uncanniness; but with the insight, one has started living in a world in which not-me has become per-sonified, very active, and very absorptive of one's weaknesses (Sullivan, 1953, p. 362).

The paranoid person starts to "project" these negative thoughts and beliefs onto the "not-me," and the dissociation increases. The paranoid transformation of the personality is beginning, and one no longer recognizes one's own negative self-evaluation and feelings of inferiority. Sullivan continues:

> Now, at the beginning of this transforma-tion, the only impression one has is of a person in the grip of horror, of uncanny devastation which makes everyone threat-ening beyond belief...it begins to put on these others—people who are outside of him, his enemies—everything which he has clearly formulated in himself as defect, blamable weakness, and so on. Thus as the process goes on, he begins to wash his

hands of all those real and fancied unfortunate aspects of his own personality which he has suffered for up to this time. Under those circumstances, needless to say, he arrives at a state which is pretty hard to remedy—by categorical name, a paranoid state (Sullivan, 1953, pp. 361-362).

Meissner (1986) describes a projective system (the unconscious projecting of oneself psychologically outside of oneself) and an introjective system (awareness of one's thoughts and feelings) and the delusional interplay between those that have formed a "paranoid construction." He writes:

The paranoid construction is equivalently a cognitive reorganization of one's experience of reality in such a fashion as to include and integrate the elements of the projective system. The function of this cognitive organization is seen most dramatically in paranoid states where an elaborate system of beliefs, attitudes, and formulations serve to justify and sustain the projective components (p. 31).

He discusses the self-representation and the external object, and the interplay between the internal (introjection) and the external (projection). The paranoid process "operates in certain ways to separate and divide us from a sense of communion and belonging with our fellow humans" (p. 32). The reciprocation between the paranoid individual and the outside world becomes what he calls the "paranoid pseudocommunity," creating:

...the persecutory bond, which is established between the paranoid individual and his persecutors or the terrifying forces that threaten him, serves as a form of paranoid construction that reinforces his projective delusions; these in turn serve to stabilize and consolidate the pathogenic sense of self that has formed itself around the core introjective configurations of victimhood and vulnerability. Thus, the victim-introject is a constant feature of these pathological expressions, yet it forms the core around which the individual's fragile sense of self is able to achieve some sense of per-durability and cohesiveness (p. 32).

Ronald K. Siegel, researching paranoia while living among paranoid individuals, writes that paranoid thinking is the outcome of one's own thinking processes that deviates from the norm and creates paranoia. As Siegel states, "...paranoid thinking could be generated by the attempt to fill in gaps between anomalous experiences, inventing coincidences and significances" (p. 195). That is, creating thoughts or beliefs about what one anticipates, but does not happen, or contradicts what one believes. And not only does Siegel believe one's thinking and beliefs create this, but also:

> ...a paranoid state resulted from a separation of the rational from the emotional brain. A paranoid's feelings are so persistent, so intense, so vivid, they make the thoughts, however deluded, seem real. Just as our normal affective feelings assure us of the reality of ourselves and the environment around us, the feelings of the paranoid assure them of their reality. When such strong feelings are unbridled by the rational brain, the

inner paranoid world becomes as believable as the real external world. Like a child who believes in monsters under the bed because he keeps seeing them in vivid night terrors, the paranoid inhabits a nightmarish world where the persistent vividness of feelings substitutes for truthfulness (Siegel, 1994, pp. 116-117).

Understanding "Meaning"

These theorists and researchers describe paranoia with fairly similar meanings but from their own theoretical viewpoints. Paranoia is a division, a separation of oneself from the outside world, but also a separation from oneself. There are many fancy psychological terms (such as projection, introjections, divided ego, homosexuality wish suppression, rational and irrational brains, and me/not-me discord) used to describe paranoia, but what is missing is the living experience of the fear, anger, suspiciousness, "hearing" others talk about them, low self-esteem, and the unacknowledged beliefs one has about oneself that are not disclosed. This current research delves into the paranoid individual's negative beliefs about themself, the derogatory statements they make to themself, and the negative thinking that supports their lack of positive self-esteem. There is more to the meaning and understanding of paranoia that has yet to be described.

As stated earlier, a definition cannot provide the meaning of an experience. Paranoia has a meaning that cannot be separated from the life of the individual experiencing it. Meaning always exists, even though we may not fully know what something or someone means to us. We can only discover "meaning" when we look between ourselves and that with which we establish meaning. We explore meaning when connecting with a person, object, or experience. We discover that a definition can differ from the actual lived-meaning of a psychological phenomenon, especially when using psychological parlance and understanding.

Meaning is the actual relationship between two people, a person and an object, or a relationship between one time of life and another. Meaning does not just exist all by itself, as if I can attach it to an experience I just happen to stumble upon. Meaning forms by participating in the relationship, event, experience, or remembered events. Fuller (1990) insightfully describes meaning this way:

> No meaning is ready-made in-itself, self-defined, able to be itself without the cooperation of anything else… Meanings exist in a network of references to one another (p. 43).

That is, meaning is created out of a relationship. Let me give you an example. When I look at my wedding ring, I remember my wife and all that my wife "means" to me, and the significant life-changing event which was my marriage. It also reminds me of my bond of marriage, children, happiness, arguments, time spent together, growing old together, sickness, health, joy, and being emotionally bonded to another person. This wedding ring is not creating this meaning, but my ring, my wife, my marital bond, and I together contribute to creating this meaning.

When I teach this subject of "meaning" in my adult psychology college classes, I look around the room for a student who has a wedding band similar to mine, and I ask them if they would be willing to exchange rings with me. The answer is always an inevitable "no." The rings look alike, but they are very different rings because each ring has helped contribute a different meaning for both of us.

This exact wedding ring of mine helps me realize the meaning I described earlier regarding my marriage. I, alone, do not create meaning. Rather, it is the relationship between me and something or someone else that forms and creates meaning. And meaning is not stagnant. The meaning also changes as people, time, events, and objects change and adjust to life's circumstances. Tillich states:

> Man's being includes his relation to meanings. He is human only by understanding and shaping reality, both his world and himself, according to meanings and values (Tillich, 1952/2000, p. 50).

Discernment of the word "*meaning*" helps us realize and better understand the meaning of paranoia as we are in the process of exploring it.

WHAT PARANOIA IS NOT

To properly address the lived-experience of paranoia and what paranoia means to the individual, I need to address what paranoia is not. Paranoia is not being in a state of confusion, panic, or plain doubt and suspiciousness, and it is not just being anxious around others. One will hear others use the word *paranoid* to describe what they are experiencing when, in fact, they are talking about a different psychological experience. People mistakenly exclaim they feel "paranoid" as a substitute for the word "fear." One may say, "I get paranoid when I drive my car in the snow," but they are talking about being "fearful" while driving in the snow.

Suppose the same statement about driving is made from a different perspective. In that case, they might say they are fearful of driving in the snow, and then their friend, standing close by, might say, "Oh, you're just being paranoid," as if paranoia is a derogatory label, a put-down that one has now attached to you to point out your worries and fears. Therefore, we can say that true *meaning* cannot be ascribed to anyone or anything by just labeling it. It is always a relationship "between."

I recently read a first-person account of a trip to the hospital because of stomach pains. This person writes, "When I feel this pain in my stomach, I get paranoid about what might be wrong with me." This is yet another example of worry or fear where the word paranoia gets substituted instead. People do not "just become" paranoid, like some mysterious foreboding cloud of paranoia has been floating around and now descends on them, and their entire personality gets momentarily altered. Paranoia is not the same as fear.

Anxiety underlies paranoia, but anxiety is not paranoia; it is not a constituent of paranoia. Many clients who go into therapy are anxious but may not be paranoid. Some paranoid clients have seen a psychiatrist before coming for therapy and may have been prescribed anti-anxiety medication, but they remain paranoid. Sullivan had an interesting way of explaining anxiety when he stated:

> People have come to hold views of themselves which are so far from valid formulations that these views are eternally catching them in situations in which the incongruity and inappropriateness are about to become evident, whereupon the person suffers the interference of anxiety. And as I have said before, when anxiety is severe, it has almost the effect of a blow on the head; one isn't really clear on the exact situation in which the anxiety occurred (Sullivan, 1953, p. 300).

As stated in the Introduction, anxiety is a prerequisite for paranoia to exist. In the eyes of most learned and enlightened individuals, anxiety exists in all aspects of life and is an "a priori" condition, existing before any mental illness has come into being. May (1983) states it thus:

> Anxiety, for example, is not an 'affect' that you can feel at some times and not at other times. It refers rather to a state of existence. It is not something we 'have,' but something we 'are' (p.77).

JOSEPH'S STORY

I believe an example of what it is like for someone who is paranoid is appropriate at this time. During a series of therapeutic sessions with Joseph, I encouraged him to explore and explain what he means when he says he is paranoid, to make it come alive for me so I know how he lives daily. I transcribed his examples and stories of being paranoid throughout his visits, with his permission. I use Joseph's story—a compilation of many discussions—not because his experience is any different from another's experience of paranoia, but because he was quite articulate in telling his story. During therapy sessions, therapists listen for the underlying foundations of paranoia and how it interferes with and negatively affects the client's personal life, relationships, and view of the world. Joseph knew he was paranoid but stated he had no control over his thoughts and feelings. Of course, if you live a paranoid existence, you already understand what Joseph is describing. If you are not paranoid, this will give you a good idea of what goes on in the world of the paranoid individual.

Joseph starts:

"I am generally known as a suspicious person. I've been anxious for years, so being both anxious and paranoid, I fear others are

watching and talking about me. When I think others are watching me, it brings all my attention onto myself, and I begin feeling like I am in a spotlight, being closely observed; every shadow in me is lit up, exposed, and explored. Why is everyone so interested in me? I can't even go outside in peace anymore because there are people out there just waiting to stare at me and talk about me.

"Why do they automatically judge me? I am becoming more scared of what others are thinking about me. I didn't always realize this, but I believe what others say about me. People are out to get me. I believe what I hear; the judgments, the condemnation, the accusations, the put-downs. I distance myself from them. I protect myself from everyone's judgments by keeping my thoughts, feelings, and beliefs to myself. I can't share with anyone because then I open myself up to further investigation and spying, and being made fun of. I feel all alone, no one to talk to that I can trust, no one cares about me. All anyone wants to do is ridicule and make fun of me. I suspect everyone, and I don't trust them anymore. I feel safer being alone. I look forward to being alone.

"Even when I have to be around other people, I keep to myself and worry about what they are thinking about me. There always seems to be someone out there who is after me and interested in finding me out, who I really am, and they want to expose me. I may not see you out there watching me, but I know you're there. Others always know where I am at all moments and know my next move before I even make it.

"Since I feel like I'm in a spotlight, other people can see into my depths and know my feelings and thoughts, the worst of my fantasies and imaginations, and that only sets me up for further mocking, scrutinization, and inspection. Now I get terrified. I don't feel safe. I want to run and escape from it all, but I can't. They keep chasing me. I can't trust anyone and must keep my secrets to myself, or I will be judged harshly. I fear so much judgment; I fear the cruelty others will impose upon me. How did this happen? What did I do to deserve this? If I can't keep myself secret anymore, I'm doomed. I can't let that happen. I will attack whoever tries to hurt me. I get

angry at anyone who I think will hurt me. I get angry every time I think about this."

Can you hear the admixture of fear and anger in Joseph's descriptions? He trusts no one, believes no one cares about him, and seeks to escape his misery. He is still trying to trust me as his therapist. Joseph is a little different from paranoid individuals who do not acknowledge their paranoia. He knows he is paranoid and is trying to work on the underlying structure that has formed his paranoid existence.

Unlike with Joseph, sometimes the therapist hears, "I am not paranoid and refuse to believe it. Those people really are out to get me." These people have become so emotionally and mentally attached to paranoia that they cannot envision themselves without it. To work on paranoia takes a lot of courage—not an absence of fear—to look paranoia in the face and say, "I need to do this. I need to get rid of my paranoia." Trust must be forged, and once it has been built and rapport established, a therapist has overcome a significant hurdle.

As described prominently throughout Joseph's description of his paranoid life, one of his fears is that others may discover his inadequacies and negative self-identity. There is a strong need for protection to keep others from seeing or spying on his weaknesses and inferiorities, which are also unacceptable to himself. It is difficult for the paranoid person to admit that they indeed believe they have faults, that they think of themself as weak and inferior and have trouble accepting themselves for who they are.

Through reciprocity, we understand that when the paranoid individual closes their blinds to others who may be outside the window looking in, they also close themself off from the world. These others, whom the paranoid individual fears are out there somewhere, do not materialize. This leaves the paranoid person believing they are helpless to defend themself against an unseen enemy and they become protective and self-preserving. This feeling of defenselessness and vulnerability is most magnified when they are alone.

Trying to eliminate these beliefs and feelings is quite difficult, as using logic, willpower, video cameras around the house, or carrying a weapon proves fruitless to lower this fear of danger. The paranoid person fears others, and fears what others will come to learn about their hidden personal secrets, and what they might just discover about themself. On and on, these negative beliefs and feelings about themself persist, years passing with no further understanding as to why they are paranoid, all for the sake of avoiding self-scrutiny, serious self-evaluation, and personal discovery. Paranoia is an attempt, albeit misguided, to remain unconscious. In many ways, it becomes an abnegation of one's individuation.

FEAR AND ANGER

Fear and anger are the predominantly experienced emotions of paranoia, especially when the perceived threats from others seem impending and imminent. As the perceived talk of the threatening other begins, the believed-to-be potential threats are felt personally, and the perceived voice of the other takes control over their life. They cannot look out yonder and always see who is observing them. Henceforth, their observer becomes what I call the "unknown-other." I use this term "unknown-other" to describe the person the paranoid individual believes is talking about or stalking them, the person "out there" who means harm, who speaks negatively and downgradingly about them, who threatens, and who is trying to expose this paranoid individual's weaknesses and vulnerabilities.

Nevertheless, an actual, real-life, physical, "observing someone" is not required for the paranoid person to hear what I call "the voice of the unknown-other." This is especially significant and intrusive when they are alone. Each of us may acknowledge a negatively evaluating, condemning self, have self-doubts, and feel inadequate to handle our present situation, but we may never take the time to reflect or recognize these deficiencies in our personality. The fear of being negatively evaluated by another person does not *create* paranoia. Paranoia is this negative self-evaluation, but also includes distrust and loneliness. *All three constituents must exist.*

Paranoid people fear being judged, so they shy away from others. They fear being intimately discovered. They do not want others to know how lonely they are, how scared they are, or how harshly others are judging them. As we will explore more thoroughly in later chapters, paranoid people fear self-discovery and admitting that what they fear about themselves may be true. Their self-beliefs are held so tightly that with any hint, any admittance, or any possibility that the slightest amount of their personal life could be revealed, they quickly protect themselves with silence, avoidance, or anger.

Are a paranoid individual's self-beliefs based on fact, truth, or real-life experience? Is everything one thinks about oneself true? Negative self-beliefs command a powerful authority, germinating enemies. One may think anything one wants about oneself or others, anything, but it does not mean it is based on fact or reality.[5,6]

---

[5] Jung: "We may call them 'imagination' or 'delusion,' but there is no 'real' thought that cannot, at times, be thrust aside by an 'unreal' one, thus proving that the latter is stronger and more effective than the former. Greater than all physical dangers are the tremendous effects of delusional ideas, which are yet denied all reality by our world-blinded consciousness. Our much vaunted reason and our boundlessly overestimated will are sometimes utterly powerless in the face of 'unreal' thoughts'" (Jung, 1969, p. 384).

[6] R. D. Laing: "A common paranoid delusion is that there is a plot directed against the self. Self attributes to others the intention to oust self from his position in the world, to displace and replace him" (Laing, 1961, p. 114).

SUMMARY

Paranoid people's lives are lonely. They feel an emotional separation between themselves and others. They may or may not be alone all the time, but they feel separated and lonely. They keep themselves isolated by physically withdrawing, and emotionally removing themselves; they do not feel part of society.

Paranoid people do not trust others well enough to feel comfortable or accepted, and they do not invite many people into their close circle. It may be acceptable to trust a parent, spouse, or best friend, but their field of trust is so limited that most people "out there" are suspect. Some paranoid individuals may be social creatures but maintain aloofness, a deep, pervasive sense of separation from others. So pervasive is this distrust that they find comfort in isolating themselves away from society where others cannot see them, judge them, or harm them. The longer they protect and isolate themselves, the more time they have to convince themselves that others are not trustworthy.

Paranoid people judge themselves negatively. They have negative self-worth, low self-esteem, and low self-image, ultimately becoming self-negating. They feel inadequate to interact with others in appropriate and meaningful ways, viewing their life as lacking, deficient, negative, worthless, and without merit, even if this is not obvious to their family and close associates. They believe others are negatively judging them. They feel scrutinized, looked down upon, observed harshly and critically, whether the persecutor is seen or not. Paranoid people do not just *think* it so; they *believe it* to their bones that others know more about their personal life than anyone should be capable of knowing, and their excessive and critical judgment grows. They believe they are judged, and they get angry at this "unknown-other" who judges so harshly and negatively. When paranoid people are angry, they use the same negative words towards themselves as they believe others use against them, which could resort to acts of violence. "Why are others so cruel and judgmental towards me?" is both belief and self-judgment of paranoia.

From this study, the three main constituents of paranoia, as discussed in this chapter, have emerged. These constituents form the basis, the structure of paranoia. A brief exploratory explanation has been given here, and I will explore each further and in greater detail in subsequent chapters. These constituents do not emerge at specific times or in a specific order through life, but all three together form what is known as paranoia.

LONELINESS

ONE CAN BE LONELY WITHOUT being paranoid, but not the other way around. There is a strong, intimate intertwining between living a lonely life and being paranoid. This chapter explores how loneliness manifests in life, how unsuccessfully overcoming loneliness interferes with the development of trusting relationships, and is an impetus toward paranoia.

The lonely person may have friends, family, and workmates, but they do not feel emotionally attached to them. They feel a distance, a gulf between themself and others that keeps them emotionally separated. They spend much of their time alone once social obligations are over. There is time to think, reflect, and stew over their loneliness. While alone, they think about this separation, this emotional distance from others, and their thoughts and feelings about themself and others turn negative. Since they are lonely, the paranoid person believes others look down on them and plot against them, and they say to themself, "All eyes are on me." They imagine others are "out there" threatening them.

THE RESEARCH

Research shows that loneliness has a great negative impact on one's physical, emotional, and mental life and is possibly at the root of many psychological problems.

> Loneliness typically refers to the feelings of distress and dysphoria resulting from a discrepancy between a person's desired and achieved levels of social relations, and there is now considerable evidence that loneliness is a risk factor for poor psychological and physical health (Cacioppo, Cacioppo, Cole, Capitanio, Goossens, & Boomsma, 2015, p. 202).

In this research on loneliness and its long-term effects, the authors noted a range of neural and behavioral effects, including:

- an increased implicit vigilance for social threats and self-defense.
- increased anxiety, hostility, and social withdrawal.
- increased sleep fragmentation and elevated vascular activity.
- increased depressed symptomatology as a non-verbal means of signaling the need for support and connection.

These effects extend beyond early developmental periods. These behavioral and neural responses may increase the likelihood of short-term survival, but they also carry long-term costs, especially when the normal life span is extended or isolation becomes chronic (Cacioppo, Cacioppo, Cole, Capitanio, Goossens, & Boomsma, 2015). It is of tremendous importance to understand loneliness and its impact, not only on the individual's emotional life and on their relationships, but how it can arouse paranoia.

LONELINESS VS. BEING ALONE

Let us start by distinguishing between loneliness and merely "being alone" and how these, working in unison, may heighten paranoia.

Loneliness is an experience on an emotional level, while being alone is a physical experience. Technically, these words, loneliness and alone, are different but are often used interchangeably. I can recognize when I am alone and when I feel lonely, but these are often experienced as the same thing by paranoid people. I refer to the word *alone* as the physical separation from others, all by oneself. When I sit in my office with the door closed, and no one else is there, I am alone, physically; no other person is within my presence in the confines of my "space." I am alone with my body, thoughts, feelings, and the current project I am pursuing. This is neither bad nor good; it is just a reality of physical space when no one else is present.

When no one else is within one's boundary or space, one is literally alone. They see themselves momentarily unattached to others. They know they are alone, and if they want this alone-ness to change, they can do something about it. One can identify one's boundaries, but they may not always be physical. One may feel uncomfortable when others stand too close or come within that imprecise measurement of comfort. With others outside of my comfort zone—my self-described comfort-measured space—I can feel just as alone as if I were in a closed room. This comfort-measured "bubble" of space is my boundary, and it is of my creation. There are many advantages to being alone. When one is by oneself, one has the time to pursue interests and hobbies. One can relax, think about one's problems, ponder on life, read, do something artistic, rehearse a speech, or occupy one's mind with stimulation such as a movie, video game, or TV. One's thoughts are one's own, and one can think and imagine whatever one wants. Many hours are spent alone while on computers.

Taking a walk in the woods where no close physical boundary exists, I am alone. There are animals, maybe some hunters far off, but the sensation of being alone is often sought while walking in the woods. As a hunter might say, being alone in nature, quiet, comfort, and peace are highly prized. The edge of the woods may be miles away, but whatever space I need at the moment to feel alone, I create; be it a shouting distance, a seeing distance, or a "feeling" distance.

When tired of being alone, one's need for companionship can be minimally satisfied by going out among strangers, going to a bar, shopping at the mall, attending a church function, or spending time with people who may have little or no personal value. When one wants to socialize again, one can reconnect with family, friends, and social activities. But there are times when one may want just another warm body with whom to share his time, thoughts, and body. Hence, aloneness ceases around others, no matter whom.

While being alone is experienced physically, loneliness is an emotional experience. The meaning of loneliness would be very difficult to understand without having first lived the life of the lonely individual. One must experience loneliness before one can understand it. Any attempt to find meaning in loneliness, if never experienced firsthand, would be an intellectual pursuit. Loneliness gains its significance through past relationships. To truly experience loneliness, one must have had a good, strong, positive relationship in the past that provided the experience of being connected, cared about, and beholden to another. This would have been a most "significant" relationship, and anyone who has had one or more significant relationships is a very lucky person indeed.

It is possible to feel alone and lonely, even when in a crowd of people. Imagine you are sitting in a diner, alone at your table, and perhaps twenty other people at their tables sitting and eating. While everyone else is eating, you feel separate, in your own bubble. The boundaries surrounding you can be great or small, but do you feel lonely? You may have a loved one at home waiting for your return after a long night at work.

With the experience of a strong, personal attachment, one feels an emotional bonding that becomes painful upon separation. During times of separation, one quickly feels and understands what it means *not* to belong, not to be connected to someone or to a group of others with whom one once shared a bond. Loneliness is the emotional separation from a relationship one had at one time.

What happens to a person when they experience this kind of separation after an extended period of togetherness? For example, a young person who has lost their friends and believes no one likes them, or an older adult who has lost their mate to death? They will experience loneliness and miss their friend/spouse with whom they have shared life. Who can fill the emotional hole left by this loss, this death?

Even in a relationship, one can feel lonely, separate, and isolated. So what is loneliness, truly, in a world of 8 billion people? How can it exist when we are linked with so many others just for our survival? Loneliness is an experience of "living-in-the-world" that does not include a significant other after having had at least one past significant and meaningful relationship. It impels a person to find a mate. Anyone who does not want to live a lonely existence seeks companionship and a willingness to share life. Loneliness can motivate one to step out of their safe surroundings and find a *"significant"* other that can assist them with what is lacking in their life. Loneliness is not a mental illness; it is an emotional separation from the attachment to another person. It is often at the root of mental illness and is at the root of paranoia. Van den Berg (1972) describes a mentally ill person (he uses the word "psychiatric") as:

> The psychiatric patient is alone. He has few relationships or perhaps no relationships at all. He lives in isolation. He feels lonely. He may dread an interview with another person. At times, a conversation with him is impossible. He is somewhat strange; sometimes he is enigmatic and he may, on rare occasions, be even unfathomable. The variations are endless, but the essence is always the same. The psychiatric patient stands apart from the rest of the world. This is why he has a world of his own (p. 105).

Contrasting a mentally and emotionally healthy individual with a psychiatric individual, Van den Berg continues:

> He is alone. He is a lonely man. Loneliness is the central core of his illness, no matter what his illness may be. Thus, loneliness is the nucleus of psychiatry. If loneliness did not exist, we could reasonably assume that psychiatric illnesses could not occur either (p. 105).

Furthermore, what can we say about someone who has never had a significant relationship in the past, has never felt loved, cared for, or believed they belonged amongst others? Would they recognize loneliness as the feeling of separation as described here, or would they only know loneliness as just another sad feeling, something they have always experienced? Some people feel lonely all the time, unable to separate feeling loneliness from their "everyday." Are "alone" and "lonely" interchangeable in their experiences? Sometimes. One can be lonely and alone, or be alone without being lonely, or be lonely among the crowd. It is important to understand that being alone differs from being lonely.

UNDERSTANDING "BELONGING"

One needs to have experienced togetherness and belonging before being able to recognize emotional separation and loneliness. When one is lonely, everyone else is "out there," and if one steps out into the crowd, will others look and wonder why they are all alone?

"What's wrong with them? Are they friendless?"

The lonely individual starts to wonder about themself, "What's wrong with me?" They protect their feelings to avoid exposing their personal life to people they do not trust. They may initially feel scared or angry when their personal space is invaded, when someone gets too close or asks too many questions. They object to others snooping around in their personal life to discover why they are lonely. The lonely and distrustful person does not want others to know anything about them.

> The person suffering from loneliness...is deeply suspicious. Even the slightest criticism hurts him. He often perceives nonexistent deprecation in surface or tangential remarks. Because he feels such grave failure in everything he undertakes, because he constantly strives to raise his level of achievement and win praise and approval and at the same time employs devices and strategies which constantly alienate him from others, eventually he either gives up or responds with aggression to cover up his inner feelings of separation, anxiety, and

despair. He is not open enough, flexible enough, expansive enough to attach himself to new persons and find value in new experiences. ...Loneliness...is a defense against an unloving world, the pain of isolation, and the yearning for tenderness and security. Underneath this defense, the individual reveals an excessive and repressed sentimentality and experiences immense anxiety that his weakness will be exposed (Moustakas, 1961, pp. 30-31).

Loneliness is a way of living *in* a relationship, albeit with an important, special someone who is no longer around. It is the absence of a significant other. The lonely person develops a longing for that someone who is not there. When their special someone is not or cannot be with them, their thoughts reach out to that person, remembering how it used to be. Loneliness has a way of drawing one into their past, and they live their feelings and emotions, not for change or motivation, but nostalgia. The emotional feeling of loneliness is an "inner" longing, a realization of feeling lonely and separate amongst others in the world, a darkness that is lived, whether with others or alone.

Through extended periods of separation, they live their life in an ever-lonely manner, away from emotional expression, even when among others. They feel trapped in their body of isolation, a vacuum through which no one hears them, isolated/ secluded by something that cannot be touched, only felt. No one is there for them. They reach out their arms for someone special, but no one receives them. They remember the hand that once held theirs.

Loneliness is a relationship of longing for the desired someone who is not there. Without a meaningful person in their life, they feel insignificant. They know they are lonely, and they disapprove of themself. Loneliness cannot be negated by just anyone or anything; it requires someone special, significant, and meaningful. It cannot be attenuated by watching television, insignificant others, or with the imagination. It cannot be escaped just by wishing it to be gone.[7]

The lonely person's thoughts retreat to his past, remembering how life used to be, but now with an increasing desire for life as it once was. It is this fleeing from feeling the present suffering of loneliness that forces them to live a life of painful loss, missing, absence, and emotional longing. Their present-day loneliness is different from the life they remember. They are not the person they remember themself to be. Yalom states it this way:

> Others combat isolation by escaping from the present, solitary moment: they comfort themselves with blissful memories of the past (even though at the time their experiences may have been far from blissful), or they project themselves into the future by enjoying the imagined spoils of as yet unrealized projects (Yalom, 1980, p. 376).

Loneliness decreases their ability to care about themself, and negative self-esteem creeps in. They degrade and blame themself for their loneliness. Over time, loneliness may become easier to tolerate, but not easier to accept. They do not view a very happy or fulfilled future (except in their fantasies), especially a future without a meaningful other. They long for what they do not have. The lonely person is afraid to think of the future, not knowing for sure if loneliness will ever end, that it could be any different someday. If they have been lonely for a long time, they worry about starting new relationships. They

---

[7] It would be most helpful to go back and reread the last three paragraphs, but instead of the words "They," "their," and "them," substitute the pronouns "I," "my," "me." These paragraphs will take on a very personal meaning.

wonder, in the event of a reprieve from loneliness, if it will return in full force when something goes wrong in their new relationship. There is no guarantee that bonding with another will ever happen. Isolation and loneliness may feel unsolvable with no one to turn to other than themself.

THE VALUE OF COMPANIONSHIP

Delving further into the meaning of loneliness, our focus now turns toward the value of togetherness and companionship, both essential to knowing and understanding loneliness. Through years of social interactions, it would not be unusual for a person to come in contact with many people with whom they have things in common. This is how friendships and work relationships happen. Some of these relationships may develop into a more romantic bonding, growing in intimacy and significance.

When we meet someone, a bond may be formed, especially if there is something particularly interesting about this other person: looks, personality, humor, artistic skill, intellect, etc. How likely is it that two people will eventually come to enjoy each other's company further after the initial meeting? What is it about the other that allows us to form a mutual relationship? This may be difficult to answer intellectually, but emotionally, a bond can form without having to know why. Examining the mutual attraction between people who have discovered something they like about the other, we notice this couple has formed an inter-relation.

If you are in a relationship yourself, you may have already analyzed what makes your relationship work. You may have figured out what supports your relationship with your partner, spouse, or friend. What does the other person contribute to this relationship, and are these mutual contributions?

To feel supported in this newly forming bond, one needs to feel respect and trust from the other. The bond may also include feeling cared about, being friends, loving each other, respecting one another, sharing, having good communication, and pursuing common interests. We may make a list of these assets within this relationship and get an idea of the *bond*, the glue of the relationship (see Fig. 1). This is a list of the "stuff" that bonds *this* relationship and helps keep *this* relationship strong. If both sides feel and believe the same items belong on this list, then this relationship is mutual.

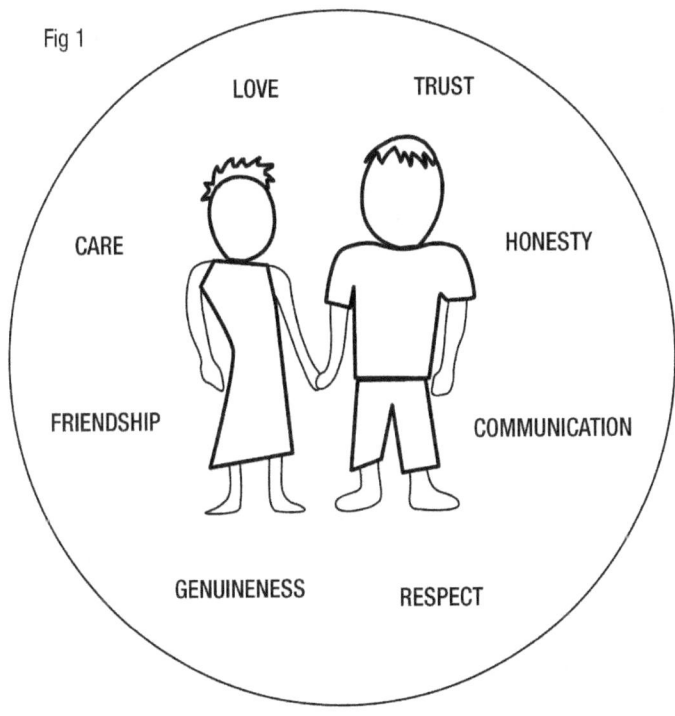

Fig 1

LOVE TRUST

CARE HONESTY

FRIENDSHIP COMMUNICATION

GENUINENESS RESPECT

The list in Fig. 1 gives a visual image that cognitively helps describe the interrelation, the glue that binds *these* two people together emotionally, physically, mentally, and spiritually. Of course, additional bonds will develop as the relationship grows.

The more people have between them, the stronger the bond can develop. I am not referring to two people who are identical in all ways, who enjoy the same things at all times, but am identifying the core values and mutual attractions—respect, caring, trust, good communication, love, etc.—that exist between them. This bond develops and grows tight in a respectful, caring, and trusting relationship.

There are, of course, other forms of relationships built on common interests that never move toward the romantic. Not all relationships are loving; some are strictly business, informal, education-based, or antagonistic. We can build bonds through common interests or group activities that bring strangers together for a while, such as a political rally, a business workshop, a college class, or church worship. Two people can differ greatly and have little in common, but when each pays attention and identifies their bonds, both can understand what helps keep them connected.

I have described a positive and meaningful bond here, a relationship that two people are comfortable in; one relies on the other and expects the other to be there more and more as they grow closer together. So let us say one person in this relationship needs to go out of town on a brief business trip, to another city to visit family, or on a hunting trip with buddies. Does this break the bonds between them? Do they lose all their connection just because of a physical separation for a while? Not necessarily. But what it will do is provide each an opportunity to experience their relationship without the other close by.

One may start to "miss" the other and realize their relationship/bond is "not together." While separated, they neither lose their trust, their respect, nor their friendship for each other, but they realize their separation. This emotional longing between them is loneliness; the separation—perhaps only temporary—is emotionally tugging at their bond. Loneliness gathers a more concise meaning through disengaged relationships, and a focus on the experience of loss through separation is required to understand loneliness at its core.

What happens to the relationship between people when these bonds are drawn out? When they experience loneliness, the bonds have become stretched, but they do not necessarily break. Each holds their end of this bond when they realize the "other" is not immediately nearby. One is alone. One reaches for that familiar hand to hold, yet that hand is not there. One speaks about something funny, but no familiar ear is there to hear it. One may still trust, but no one trustworthy is right there at their side. This is loneliness.

What if loneliness does not end in a few days (see Fig. 2), or one's friend does not return? What if other circumstances, such as death, have created this distance between oneself and the other? In the experience of long-term or extreme separation, one feels no one is there for them any longer, and this becomes painfully intolerable. If it goes on substantially long, then loneliness seems never to end; they wonder if it may become permanent, that no one will *ever* be there for them again.

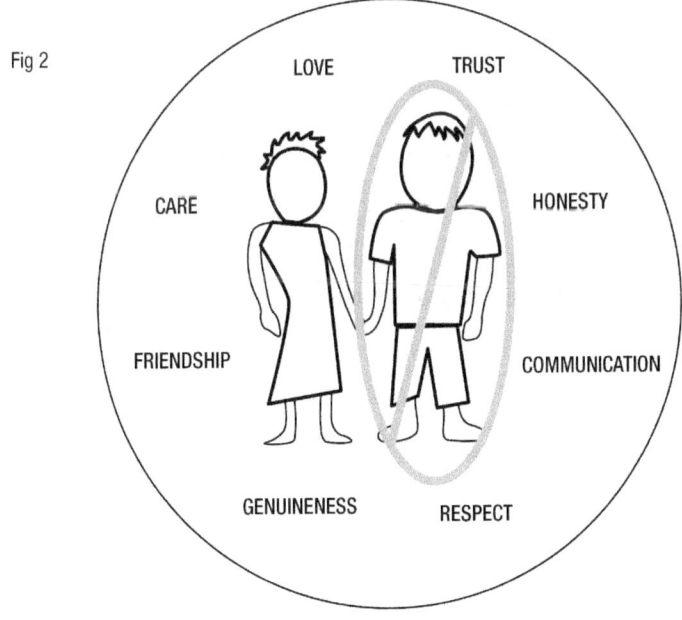

Fig 2

LOVE TRUST

CARE HONESTY

FRIENDSHIP COMMUNICATION

GENUINENESS RESPECT

Without a significant, important other, one grows increasingly lonely. Loneliness and isolation provide the fuel for increasingly negative self-talk, self-deprecation, and distrust of others. When a person has no one to talk to for an extended time, one starts talking to oneself with increasing tolerance for illogic, incorrect assumptions, distrust, fear, and suspicion. Van den Berg states:

> The reason for this is that the healthy person will discover in his healthy fellowmen the selfsame, or more or less the same, conversions, projections, transferences and distortions of memory as he himself has, whereas the mentally ill person is alone with his mental mechanisms (van den Berg, 1972, p. 105).

Even a monk or nun must contend with loneliness since their kind of self-imposed isolation does not automatically create paranoia.[8] Loneliness is not necessarily prevented through human contact, as we have described above, but having another person close by allows the lonely individual to talk about their feelings, explore their life more fully, possibly learn to develop trust, adjust their thoughts and beliefs to a more peer-review level, and may get them out among others more often to explore what they won't do by themself.

It is probably easy to imagine being home alone for a day with no one to talk to. How about a week? What happens if

---

[8] Please see The Collected works of St. John of the Cross and Teresa of Avila for examples of how religious individuals have dealt with their isolation. "The Inward Solitude" in *No Man Is an Island* by Thomas Merton addresses how cloistered individuals can effectively deal with their loneliness and isolation. Also, see the chapter "Existential Isolation and Psychotherapy" in *Existential Psychotherapy* by Ivan D. Yalom.

being alone extends to months? The paranoid individual does not have anyone close to him, anyone significant enough to bond through trust and respect, no mutual and respected companionship. I am not talking about just a few days without a friend, a few weeks alone when someone has gone away with the probability of return; I am talking about *years* going by without friendships, with no mutual bonding and no comfortable feeling that someone significant is there.

For many reasons, the paranoid person distances and estranges themself from others. For them, they are alone in a very real physical sense, and emotionally, they are lonely. As their paranoia grows, they may live among others but still feel lonely, not believing anyone understands them or cares about them, with an increasing sense of suspiciousness.

Anytime there is a break in a significant relationship, loneliness is possible. Most times, once one has recovered from loss enough to reach out to another person, loneliness can find its cure. Is it necessary to trace one's loneliness into the past to understand it completely, or is it only important to examine loneliness at the moment of separation? Tracing one's frequency of loneliness can be helpful to understand better how one has dealt with loneliness in the past or if one has become trapped in a repeating pattern, i.e., a chronic victim of loneliness.

STAYING IN THE PRESENT

What do we do during our lonely time? Even when we are lonely, we still have decisions to make about life. Loneliness opens up our present life to other possibilities. We can live our loneliness in the present moment and learn to count on ourselves; we cannot always count on others being there. Are we failing to live any aspect of our life that was being fulfilled by a significant other?

When lonely, we live with our memories of the past and do not view a better future for ourselves. All we have is the present time to delve into our lives, understand ourselves and our lack of relationships, and explore interests, hobbies, talents, and other possibilities. We can take the time now to learn more about ourselves and see if a better future can exist, even with loneliness. Moustakas gives us a sensitive, heartfelt example of his loneliness while experiencing his young daughter's hospitalization, and he took that opportunity to look into "the heart of the lonely experience." He writes:

> ...I began to discover the meaning of loneliness. I began to see that loneliness is neither good nor bad, but a point of intense and timeless awareness of the Self, a beginning which initiates totally new sensitivities and awarenesses, and which results in bringing a person deeply in touch with his own existence and in touch with others in a fundamental sense. I began to see that in the deepest experiences the human being can know—the birth of a baby, the prolonged illness or death of a loved relative, the loss of a job, the creation of a poem, a painting, a symphony, the grief of a fire, a flood, an accident—each in its own way touches upon the roots of loneliness. In each of these experiences, in the end, we must go alone.

> In such experiences, inevitably one is cut off from human companionship. But experiencing a solitary state gives the individual the opportunity to draw upon untouched capacities and resources and to realize himself in

an entirely unique manner. It can be a new experience. It may be an experience of exquisite pain, deep fear and terror, an utterly terrible experience, yet it brings into awareness new dimensions of self, new beauty, new power for human compassion, and a reverence for the precious nature of each breathing moment (Moustakas, 1961, pp. 6-7).

If we stay in the here and now, we "feel" what it means to experience loneliness. We may hope not to be lonely someday, but it is between the present moment and this "someday" that we have the opportunity to prepare our lives for something more. Living loneliness in the present moment allows us to plan for the day when we will no longer be lonely. We cannot force another person to love, respect, or show concern for us, but we can prepare ourselves for its possibility. Even if another person comes into our life showing care and concern, there remains no guarantee of the other's continued participation in our life. The ending of loneliness is a commitment to our present and to our preparation for something better someday. The feeling of loneliness can leave us in an instant, yet how or when this may occur remains unpredictable. We are obligated to find the inner strength and desire to do something just for ourselves for a while, for loneliness may not always be there.

Not only the paranoid individual, but we all have the right to think and believe as we want, to feel, imagine, create, or stupefy as we wish. We can absorb and learn new things, or the opposite; we can hypnotize ourselves by binge-watching TV shows and playing video games. When alone, I keep my thoughts to myself. I do not have to share my thoughts and feelings with anyone. If I want to believe that the sky is green, I can. If I want to believe someone "out there" wants to hurt me, that I am estranged, not wanted, not loved, or that no one cares about me or understands me, I can believe it. These are *my* beliefs. I have a right to my beliefs, my privacy, and my silence. R. D. Laing makes this interesting observation about the paranoid individual:

> When one gets to know such a person more than superficially, one often discovers that what tortures him is not so much his delusions of reference, but his harrowing suspicion that he is of no importance to anyone, that no one is referring to him at all.

> What constantly preoccupies and torments the paranoid is usually the precise opposite of what at first is most apparent. He is persecuted by being the centre of everyone else's world, yet he is preoccupied with the thought that he never occupies first place in anyone's affection (Laing, 1961, p. 118).

THE IMPACT OF LONELINESS

The paranoid person is lonely and often prefers to be alone. Being alone and lonely presents them with increased opportunities to listen to their thinking and self-judgments. This individual seldom shares their thoughts and beliefs with anyone. There is usually no one around to share their thoughts, but they also distrust others, preferring not to share their thoughts. They think and believe their thoughts, alone, and that fuels paranoia. Paranoia feeds on loneliness and isolation.

Paranoia takes the lonely person's thoughts and compounds and confounds them. They believe their conceived judgments just because they think them. They catch someone glancing their way, and they think, "That person is staring at me," thus making the paranoid individual believe their thought is in fact true, that it matches reality, and, being uncertain as to any other possibility of what the other's look may mean. They believe they are being observed and judged, and others are threatening; "That person wants to hurt me," they think. Being lonely for too long gives their thoughts more power than they can deal with through reasonable circumspection. If these unsubstantiated beliefs and thoughts are not exposed and corrected through interaction and open dialogue with others, "Who else is out there threatening me?" becomes the thought that follows.

CHILDREN AND LONELINESS

An introverted child tends to be quieter than an extroverted child; they keep more of their thoughts and feelings to themself. What if the child is extremely introverted and does not share their feelings or thoughts with anyone? As silence increases, so does the child's fantasy, imagination, and delusional life, all of which can keep them removed from social situations and friendships.

> ...one can make shocking mistakes and get oneself laughed at, punished, and so on, for reporting what we call lively fantasy as real phenomena, If only because that in itself can be so disconcerting, a 'lonely' child has a natural bent toward social isolation, which is one of the relatively unfortunate outcomes of the next era of development (Sullivan, 1953, p. 225).

Loneliness can become habitual if the child cannot find their way out of loneliness. Parents and other providing adults may not know the child is lonely. Depending on the socialization skills not acquired, the child may be hindered from developing close, meaningful future friendships.

Parents know children talk to themselves—private speech—when they are young. Listen closely, and you can hear the young child talk about their problems, argue with others who are not there, try out new, braver ways of solving their conflicts, and talk like their parents. Until they are interrupted, they may not know they have been talking to themself. This private speech eventually turns inward with age. The child stops talking aloud and entertains their personal, private speech within their thinking; now, no one else can hear them.

No research or data suggests private speech leads to paranoia, but by understanding private speech, one gets a clearer distinction between open dialogue with other human beings and the dialogue one maintains within oneself. When alone or lonely, they have no one else to talk to concerning deep and personal matters, and so they tend not to share their thoughts. Without the help of others, the child attempts to figure out their problems alone. A lonely child only consults with themself, and if something scares, angers, or confuses them, they make sense of it with what they have: their beliefs, fantasies, and imagination. Siegel believes:

> ...a paranoid state resulted from a separation of the rational from the emotional brain (Siegel, 1994, p. 116).

When a child has no one to talk to about their thoughts, feelings, beliefs, fears, anxieties, or biological urges, they become less rational and more prone to fantasy and turn to their imagination when looking for intimacy and cognizance.

ISOLATION IN CHILDHOOD

As contrasted with a healthy personality, the development of a paranoid personality is one peril of growing up lonely and isolated from others, especially within one's age group. Sullivan wrote of the developmental phase of pre-adolescence as an exceedingly important period in a child's life by stressing the crucial necessity of developing friendships. He discusses the friendship he called "the chum," a same-sex friend who helps form a very grounded and bonded "intimacy."

Through this friendship, young boys can identify and learn firsthand what it means to be a boy through non-sexual intimacy with another male. By playing, talking, and interacting, together they make sense of the world, growing up, talking to girls, and learning to develop the confidence to share feelings, worries, fears, and their fantasy life without the fear of retribution or being ostracized. The importance of good, honest, meaningful relationships cannot be underestimated when children are vulnerable concerning the roots of paranoia.

Sullivan maintains that because of this corrective influence of the 'chum,' many individuals avoid serious mental disorders (Muuss, 1996, p. 98).

To emphasize the importance of age-related friendships, Muuse gives us an account of what loneliness can do to a child:

> Since human beings are basically social creatures, they experience throughout life a recurrent need to be with others. This need may take on various qualities and involve numerous people, including imaginary playmates; nevertheless, to seek contact with others remains a powerful force at all ages. The infant craves tenderness and physical contact, the child wants adult participation in play activities, the juvenile has a need for compeers, the preadolescent craves a chum, and the adolescent pines for sexual intimacy and love.

The lack of satisfying personal contacts is experienced as loneliness, which the individual feels with great intensity during pre-adolescence and which, later in life, may become even more terrible than anxiety. Although the lonely child often has a rich fantasy life, this may contribute to social isolation, which increases anxiety about the process of seeking companionship. In the juvenile era, reporting one's fantasies to peers can invite ridicule, ostracism, and avoidance, all of which tend to perpetuate social isolation. This leads to more fantasy and creates a vicious circle that discourages a reality orientation vis-à-vis other people and contributes to the derailment of the socialization process (Muuss, 1996, p. 99).

EXAMPLES OF PARANOIA

Here, I will use three examples of individuals who describe being lonely and acknowledge they are paranoid. Two were adolescents when I first met them, and the third was a middle-aged adult. Two described having a social life, i.e., they had people around them and someone who cared about them. Their loneliness seemed to be associated with low self-esteem or a personal trauma that they alone could not work through. Although they had others around, the increase in isolation propelled them toward paranoia.

Peter, from our Introduction, says he knew he was paranoid a couple of years before he came to counseling at age sixteen. He says he felt very different from others, had been a loner for a few years, and often secluded himself in his house. He dropped out of high school when he turned sixteen. Peter recalls having a lot of friends and being a very active, sports-motivated child. He was a star on his elementary and junior high school basketball teams, and he also excelled in academics.

He did not know why, but when he was about eleven years old, he felt different from his friends, a distance developed between them. He lost interest in basketball because he no longer wanted to be the center of attention and dropped off the team. Others told him he was good at basketball, "But I didn't believe them anymore." His grades suffered. He says he felt embarrassed about doing poorly now in school. He started feeling lonely. He did not want affection from anyone, but he did not know why.

"I just wanted to be left alone. I became scared to be around people. I believed they were talking about me." As Peter recalled growing into adolescence, he avoided close relationships. He did not trust people, not sure what they wanted from him. He says, "When I'm alone, I can protect myself and my feelings from being hurt. Yeah, I'm lonely, but that's easier than being scared all the time and not trusting anyone." He thought to himself, "Who could love me?"

Even when his mother said she loved him, Peter did not believe her. He says that feeling lonely, wanting companionship but being too scared to try, and not understanding why he detached from people still bothers him, but admits he still craves friendship.

BETTY

My next example is Betty, who is now twenty years old, paranoid, and still believes she must stay distant from others because of her distrust and suspicion. She has no close friends. When she was about 9 or 10 years old, she started believing she was not as pretty as the other girls. She was teased because she was a little heavier. She remembers telling herself, "You can't hang out with those girls; they don't like you." She remembers feeling lonely after that, not being able to open up and talk about herself with anyone else.

Her mother was a drug addict, not physically or emotionally available, as Betty recalls, so she decided to face her life alone, just putting up a good front and not making waves that could get her noticed. She spent the next several years avoiding interpersonal contact as much as possible. She learned to take care of herself and not depend on others.

Healthy relationships counteract loneliness and low self-esteem. But what if a child has no chum/friend, no positive adult influences, is too anxious to be around others, or has such a low opinion of themselves that they believe no one else cares about them? Erikson writes:

> Young people can also be remarkably clannish, and cruel in their exclusion of all those who are "different," in skin color or cultural background, in tastes and gifts, and often in such petty aspects of dress and gesture as have been temporarily selected as *the* signs of an in-grouper or out-grouper. It is important to understand (which does not mean condone or participate in) such intolerance as a defense against a sense of identity confusion. For adolescents not only help one another temporarily through much discomfort by forming cliques and by stereotyping themselves, their ideals, and their enemies; they also perversely test each other's capacity to pledge fidelity (Erikson, 1950/1963, p. 262).

Loneliness can become pervasive at this young age and in the following years. The younger child and teen need others to talk with, communicate their needs and struggles, and feel welcomed. That does not always happen. The adolescents I used as examples did not feel prepared for the social world and were coming to terms with their need to "go it alone." Both convinced themselves that no one was there for them, that they could no longer trust anyone, and that others were threatening. Loneliness had become their life and had set them up for paranoia.

Let us now look at the third example, an adult who developed paranoia after years of what one might call "normal" growth and development well into middle age.

While fully immersed in therapy, Roman remembered being an extroverted child; he liked people, had many friends, and enjoyed playing soccer, football, and baseball into his adulthood. He made a good living as an accountant for a car dealership. Being somewhat bombastic, he often boasted about his accomplishments in the past regarding previous lovers, sports awards, and his keen sense of humor. He loved his wife and children, provided well for them, and enjoyed going to work daily. He strongly emphasized that he used to participate fully in his life.

At some point, the company he worked for started doing "shady" financial practices, actions that eventually got the company in trouble with the IRS. Roman initially refused when he was instructed to "fix the books" so the company could cover up their unethical doings; he was told he would be fired if he did not comply. Roman still had three teenage children to support, so he went along with the company's fraudulent request. The regulating agency overseeing this kind of business discovered the illegal activities, and the company blamed Roman for doing all this on his own. He was fired. Many lawsuits followed.

This devastated Roman and he felt stigmatized by what had happened to him: fired from his job, his honesty being questioned, his self-esteem shot, his embarrassment for what others must think of him. He started avoiding people and became emotionally distant from his wife, children, and friends. He believed he could no longer work at any job or be around people. He did not want to go out of the house. Roman was afraid of what others were now thinking about him. He no longer trusted people and believed that "everyone" was now out to get him and judge him for what he did.

Roman kept the blinds drawn tight so no one would know he was home. Feelings of loneliness now pervaded Roman's life to the point where he withdrew from society and was now unwilling to be around others. He still wished to have friendships the way he did before all this started, but he now believed others were incapable of seeing him as a trusted friend. He sat and watched TV all day. He became more and more paranoid.

A Constituent of Paranoia

Loneliness is a decisive constituent of paranoia, as we have been discussing. It is not necessarily a childhood issue but can start at any age. In this study of paranoia, we are not looking for "causes" of paranoia, but are discovering the underlying roots that make paranoia what it is. Loneliness does not create paranoia; it is one integral aspect of paranoia. Nor does loneliness have to be the first in a sequence of life struggles that bring paranoia into existence.

1. Paranoia does not just develop after 1-2-3—loneliness, distrust, and poor self-esteem—emerge in ascending order. There is no ordered timeline of events that sequentially come together to form paranoia. All constituents are already in place for paranoia to be paranoia, and recognizing loneliness as one aspect of paranoia helps us identify one of the deep and personal issues that support paranoia.
2. How to help the paranoid person better understand what is at the core of this common human condition.
3. The need for developing a trusting and supportive relationship with the paranoid individual.

The development of paranoia is fraught with loneliness, but to be clear, this does not mean every example of loneliness results in paranoia.

Summary

In summary, when one is alone, one experiences the human capacity to experience life outside the presence of other people, to have one's body separated from the presence of others. Loneliness is the emotional, temporary, or possibly permanent lack of, or separation from, a significant other. Loneliness is a necessary experience for paranoia to exist. With extended periods of isolation and loneliness, one believes others are threatening. One is suspicious of who may be scheming and plotting against them.

> Almost everyone has had a mild experience such as the vague suspicion that *something* is out there just waiting to get us. Darkness and solitude invite the feeling. Many people experience it when they are alone in the house at night or walk down an unfamiliar street. Others may have the vague feeling that their life paths are being jeopardized by jealous persons known or unknown. The creature we all fear, the demon of paranoia, is not "out there," but lurking in the shadows of our very own brains (Siegel, 1994, p. 7).

From the psychological viewpoint, the ongoing and continual emotional experience of loneliness participates in one's developing paranoia. Loneliness is just one aspect, one essential, integral component. We are now prepared to look at the others.

DISTRUST

T HE INABILITY TO TRUST PEOPLE is a constituent, a component aspect of paranoia. As mentioned earlier, a constituent is part of the essence of whatever phenomenon we are examining, in our case, *paranoia*. Constituents are not a result of cause and effect, but they are fundamental for this phenomenon to exist *as* this phenomenon. Distrust of others does not, all by itself, create paranoia, but when we examine paranoia in greater depth, along with its other constituents, we find distrust is integral to what paranoia is.

I will discuss what it means to "distrust" but limit the discussion to interpersonal relationships, not whether one group trusts another group, or in institutions such as country, government, or religion. I will investigate how trust is a fundamental aspect of life, confidence in our interaction with others, and how it is a necessary foundation for significant interpersonal relationships. Without trust, one's relationships may be built on something else—something not as sturdy, e.g., aloofness, hate, power, deception, manipulation, or antagonism. I will show how the paranoid individual lives his life devoid of trust and how this confounds and negatively influences his relationships.

UNDERSTANDING TRUST

What does it *mean* to trust someone, and does trust have a deeper meaning? Trust may take years to develop, but the sad part is that it can be destroyed in an instant. Can trust be repaired once it is broken?

> Trust is at the centre of a whole web of concepts: reliability, predictability, expectation, cooperation, goodwill, and–on the dark side–distrust, insincerity, conspiracy, betrayal, and incompetence (Hawley, 2012, p. 3).

So begins our search into what trust means, how we recognize it, whether we can trust our ability to trust, and if trust can be fixed or repaired once it is broken. Non-paranoid people may find it easier to trust people, but they also may decide not to trust certain individuals when necessary, possibly because of broken promises or contentious events from their past. This does not automatically make them paranoid. Some people can trust a stranger immediately and will continue doing so until that person proves themself to be untrustworthy. Others are very cautious and will not automatically trust, but will wait until one proves within a reasonable assurance that they are trustworthy.

Being able to trust or distrust is not automatically necessary in relationships between two people. One can develop trust over time through experience and proof. One may demonstrate honesty through words and behavior, that a verbal contract will be fulfilled as promised, that one's handshake is a commitment, and that one's word is one's honor. As the old saying goes, "A man is only as good as his word, and no more," which is equally true for women. In the interpersonal, I trust that my wife will always love me and that my children will always be where they say they will be when they leave the house. I trust my clients to be as honest with me as possible. If I tell a secret, I trust my friends will keep that secret. I trust my doctor since I have known him for several years, even though I know nothing about his personal life.

Sometimes one must take a risk to trust the other, such as an emergency room doctor, a teacher, an officer of the law, or a spiritual advisor. With trust, one can commit to others, even if that commitment is not spelled out or written in contract form.

Trust has much to do with how we live our own life, mainly through honesty, responsibility, commitment, integrity, and respect. Trust and honesty are synonymous. We have much to gain by being trustworthy besides integrity and authentic self-esteem. Opening oneself up psychologically, one is vulnerable about how one lives, deciding whether the risk is worth it. To open myself up to being trustworthy is a commitment I make to others. Trusting others is a risk, and am I willing to take that risk?

Trust is a commitment to someone else's future as well. One must have integrity and honesty if making a promise to another, not just in this beginning moment but ongoing until the commitment is complete. When someone trusts me, I must commit to completing what I have promised. I must be able to say "yes, I can," or "no, I can't," honestly, without the intention of deceiving.

> Trust benefits those who receive it, and distrust is a harm; conversely, there are many advantages to getting it right about (un) trustworthiness for those who offer trust. When others depend upon us, our decisions regarding trust have far-reaching consequences, consequences we should take into account as best we can. This is why trust and trustworthiness matter in inter-

personal relationships, and for our everyday lives (Hawley, 2012, p. 18).

While I may be honest and trustworthy, there is no guarantee that other people are honest and that they will reciprocate
my trust. These last few paragraphs may sound confusing since
they touch on several aspects of trust from different perspec-
tives, but the importance of trust is that it forms the basis, from
both directions, for forming a good, strong interpersonal and
mutual relationship. We must take trust seriously.

MEANING OF TRUST

How can we ascertain the *meaning* of trust? As we have discussed in an earlier chapter, we cannot find meaning in the
word's definition. Meaning is the relationship between one person and another or a relationship between a person and something else; we should start by understanding the meaning of
trust as a *relationship*. I alone do not define this meaning, but I
am a part of it.

When I ask young children how they understand what
trust means, they say that if they have a secret and tell their
friend, their friend will tell no one else. That is how they know
they can trust their friend. So young children learn whom they
can trust, and also who not to trust, but sometimes they get it
wrong. Trust among young friends is fickle at best. Children
benefit from exploring trust and learning about it from their
"best" friends. They also benefit from having a strong, trusting
adult to teach them about trust. Adolescents say a good trusting
friend is one who will not "stab them in the back (figuratively),"
will keep their secrets, is honest and will not spread lies, will not
turn their backs on them, and will not kick them out of their
social group.

Adults will add to this understanding of being trustworthy as someone who can be counted on when needed, who is honest and will fulfill a commitment, and who will help them and be there for them in times of discord, suffering, and need. Trust is the ability to believe what another says is true, and that one can rely on another's integrity, reliability, honesty, and truth.

To be precise, we cannot say that trust is the foundation of *all* relationships, since it is not the foundation of antagonistic, suspicious, or hate-filled relationships. There are also relationships, such as those built on money, sex, addiction, work environment, or rancor, all of which do not require trust to maintain. But trust is the foundation of meaningful and significant interpersonal relationships that gives this bond its strength, especially one that is also supported by love, caring, respect, communication, genuineness, and honesty. Paranoid people seldom develop relationships that involve interpersonal trust. They rarely trust their close family members, and this distrust can grow stronger over the years.

"Trust" in Relationships

Relationships are strengthened by trust and other potential interpersonal qualities. We can examine the bonds of a relationship for their strengths and weaknesses, and whether they are mutual. Relationships built on a solid grounding of trust will withstand great forces that attempt to tear them apart. Meaningful romantic, interpersonal relationships are built upon a foundation of trust, a metaphorical solid concrete slab as a supportive structure (See Fig. 3). A strong, solid, sound foundation can support relationships through good and bad, for better or worse, in sickness and in health. Trust is this foundation, this structure, the solidness upon which one can build relationships. A relationship that has trust as its foundation has confidence and stability.

Many types of human relationships are not built on or require trust as part of the relationship, but for loving, caring, supportive, long-term relationships, trust provides the strength to build and rest. Trust *is* the foundation of solid, loving relationships. Without trust, any attempt to build an interpersonal, supportive relationship is like building on sand—unsteady, fraught with dangers and uncertainty—and there is the ominous possibility of collapse. Distrust becomes a crack in a once-solid foundation, splitting from within, jeopardizing its solidness and ability to hold and withstand weathering through tough times.

Once trust is broken, there is no repairing it. We witness this in marriages leading to divorce. A foundation that is patched is still weak. It may look good and appear strong from the outside, but those cracks are still there; the potential collapse remains. When the next emotional storm comes, those cracks open again. An interpersonal and loving relationship not built on trust is not solid and will not support or hold up under pressure.

The only way to fix a trust-broken bond, whose relationship's foundation has been damaged or destroyed, is to start over. The foundation needs to be rebuilt, go back to the ground, and again begin building mutual and common support within this relationship and re-establish trust as the new foundation. Broken trust cannot be repaired, but the damaged relationship can begin anew by building upon a new, solid foundation of trust.

Attempts can be made to revitalize this foundation. Wipe clean all that was at one time the foundation of the now-damaged relationship and start building again. In an interpersonal relationship, the couple needs to start talking again, identify the dishonesty, promise never to deceive again, start rebuilding trust, practice honesty, and reestablish what had been destroyed by dishonesty, lies, and deception. Couples must start over with trust and do everything they can to strengthen this new relationship. They will quickly learn if trust is possible between them and if each is willing to start building again.

With business partners (which can be an intimate relationship), each will need to redefine their relationship to include trust, honesty, and mutual purpose. A child that has broken their parents' trust will need to promise to work at rebuilding their relationship with them. This new, required promise must include stopping the lies, always being where they say they will be, helping around the house, talking about their struggles with honesty, and giving their parents plenty of time to believe that honesty and trust can exist again.

To rebuild trust, one needs to start over and begin again. A relationship built upon this new trust foundation can be strong. Stopping the lies, cheating, distortions, backstabbing, name-calling, and uncaringness can work toward forming a solid relationship that can grow and develop into something meaningful. As trust builds, memories of past indiscretions need to fall away and be forgiven.

ERICKSON'S STAGES OF DEVELOPMENT: TRUST VS. MISTRUST

Trust is not only the basis of good supportive interpersonal relationships; it also influences the structure and support of one's individual life from the earliest developmental stage. Before the child is even conscious of itself, with or without trust in its foundation, the child grows with strengths and dysfunctions through future phases of development, all being tinged by trust's absence or inclusion. From Erikson's psychosocial theory, we learn infants develop an ability to trust from their earliest experiences with their caregivers. We will only focus on the first of Erikson's eight stages of development, trust vs. mistrust. As Muuss states:

> Each of the eight developmental stages is characterized by a conflict, and each conflict contains the possibility of bipolar outcomes. Erikson suggests that the individual must actually experience both sides of the conflict and must learn to subsume them into higher synthesis. ...If the conflict is worked out in a constructive, satisfactory manner, the syntonic or positive quality becomes the more dominant part of the ego and enhances further healthy development through the subsequent stages. ...However, if the conflict persists past its time, or is resolved unsatisfactorily, the dystonic or negative quality is incorporated into the personality structure. In that case, the dystonic or negative attribute will interfere with future development and may manifest itself in impaired self-concept, adjustment problems, and possibly, psychopathology (Muuss, 1996, p. 46).

57

If caregivers are sensitive to the infant's needs, providing food and positive stimulation when needed, nurturing, caring, and reducing anxiety-provoking stimulation, the infant develops trust and confidence in those around him, possibly expanding this gained trust to the rest of the world. Erikson states:

> Mothers create a sense of trust in their children by that kind of administration which in its quality combines sensitive care of the baby's individual needs and a firm sense of personal trustworthiness within the trusted framework of their culture's lifestyle. This forms the basis in the child for a sense of identity, which will later combine a sense of being "all right," of being oneself, and of becoming what other people trust one will become (Erikson, 1950/1963, p. 249).

The opposite would also be true, that distrust develops if care is not sensitive, if the child goes hungry beyond reason, if no one comforts or provides positive and adequate stimulation, or if abuse enters this infant's life. According to psychosocial theory, the ability to trust develops early on, and its effects, both positive and negative, grow with the child into the subsequent stages of development, each stage building upon what has been set in motion in previous stages.

Erikson focused on the mother and her ability to raise and care for her infant adequately and with sensitivity, but mothers are not the only caregivers in today's world. Many infants are now being raised by grandparents, babysitters, or daycare staff, all of whom are now "substitutes" for the care that was once mostly provided by the mother. If there is an early development of trust, along with confidence, resiliency, strong ego development, and strength of will, then the foundation for life is strong, confident, resilient, and able to weather the difficulties and stress of life well into the future. Trust is an empowering foundation for life itself, not just in a one-to-one personal relationship.

TRUST IN CHILDHOOD

What are we trying to do when we establish a family foundation for raising strong, healthy, trusting children? What are *our* intentions as caregivers, and how do we attempt to accomplish this goal? It depends on how we think about foundations and their purpose. As before, using the metaphor of a concrete slab as the life foundation for a child, with adequate love, trust, care, discipline, and taking the time necessary to make the child feel wanted and accepted, a good solid foundation is being built for this child's future.

Even when reprimand, restrictions, guidance, and limitations are necessary, the solidness of this foundation is not negatively affected, as long as the discipline is done with care and supportive child-rearing practices. Pressure is exerted on this foundation under the strain of child abuse, authoritarian upbringing, excessive spoiling and leniency, or abandonment. Cracks form in this child's developmental foundation. The life being built is now on faulty underpinnings, and a foundation that is not solid is weak and may eventually crumble.

While raising children, parents are often confronted with the question, "What is the best way to discipline my child?" Do parents need authoritarian control and domination over their child's life, complete control over every decision the child makes? Do they need to be, and enjoy being, helicopter parents? Are they trying to break their child's spirit and encourage dependence upon the parents and society?

The parents need to figure out why they want to raise children and their goals (the parents') for raising children. Older methods, such as physical punishment, have been replaced in more modern times by grounding and restriction, talking with the child regarding right and wrong choices, and positive reinforcement to encourage good, moral behavior. If parents want to create a dependent, angry young adult, the use of permissive or authoritarian parenting will provide that.

The permissive parenting style encourages immaturity and a lack of responsibility and blocks honest personal reflection in the child. An eventual delusion emerges that others and the world will provide for all the child's needs and wants as they have become accustomed. Authoritarian parenting promotes strict discipline, distrust, fear, and revenge on the world. The question when raising children should be, "What is it that I want to accomplish?"

Through Miller, we find examples of different parenting styles, and as she points out, many can have cruel, devastating effects on the child. However, by recognizing the purpose of discipline while raising children—with the ultimate goals, we hope, of love, support, trust, and genuine care—we learn the noble purpose and responsibility of parenting. Miller says it this way:

> For children need a large measure of emotional and physical support from the adult. This support must include the following elements if they are to develop their full potential:
>
> - Respect for the child.
> - Respect for their rights.
> - Tolerance for their feelings.
> - Willingness to learn from their behavior:
>   - About the nature of the individual child.
>   - About the child in the parents themselves.
>   - About the nature of emotional life, which can be observed much more clearly in the child than

in the adult because the child can experience his feelings much more intensely and, optimally, more undisguisedly than an adult (Miller, 1983, p. 100).

Trust in Adulthood

Sometimes we adults are leery when it comes to trusting. We may not know someone well enough to trust, and we respond with reservation. If we determine this person is trustworthy, we feel a little more confident in trusting them again in the future. It may still be possible to trust some people with just a handshake or a verbal agreement; their word is as good as their agreement. Interactions of one person with another will involve various degrees of trust. Some people immediately trust others, not knowing if the other person is trustworthy. These people just assume the other is trustworthy. Some will trust others just a little at a time, "test the water," so to speak. Over time, if trust seems warranted, then they try trusting more often and possibly build a trusting relationship.

But some non-paranoid people do not trust and will trust no one until they have enough proof that the other person is trustworthy, which requires a great deal of proof and evidence. They are not readily willing to give anyone a trusting chance. If the possibility of trust in a newly forming relationship can exist:

1. It can occur right away until proven false.
2. No trust will exist until enough proof over time has happened for the other to be declared trustworthy.

Is it good to trust too quickly? Maybe yes, and maybe no. Sometimes trust is important, even if one does not fully understand or know the other person. Through her in-depth study on trust, Hawley discusses various states of trust and distrust,

61

and the difficulty of knowing whether trust is appropriate in all situations. She states:

> Trusting or distrusting doesn't always feel like something we choose to do—very often, we simply find ourselves in a state of trust or distrust, with little awareness of how we have arrived there. So what's the point of thinking about who we should trust, if trusting lies beyond our control? ...Trusting someone to do something is often a matter of believing they are trustworthy in the relevant respect. When trust involves belief, it is no surprise that it lies beyond our direct control: I cannot simply decide to believe you are trustworthy. Even when I trust you without fully believing you to be trustworthy, my evidence places some constraints on my trust. If I firmly believed you were totally untrustworthy, it's hard to see how I could trust you in any respect. I might be able to pretend to trust you, to behave in public as if I trust you. But actual trust would be beyond my reach (Hawley, 2012, pp. 78-79).

For example, if you are due to have surgery, it helps to trust your doctor even if you've never met before needing an operation. A good doctor will try to develop trust quickly with a new patient. Patients will probably feel better about having an operation when they trust the surgeon and are expecting a complete recovery. What belief or attitude towards recovery do you think one would have if they did not or could not trust their doctor? Do you trust your boss, police officers, teachers, and your spouse? Some of these situations of trust are not decided beforehand.

Sometimes we must trust, even if there is a minute possibility that the other person is not to be trusted. Trust, in itself, is neutral. It only becomes important between people,[9] and that is the tricky part; when to trust, and how to know *if* we can trust. Trust establishes meaning within relationships. The first thing we must do to develop trust in interpersonal relationships is to get to know the other person very well. As we learn about this person in as many areas of life and varying situations, it will be easier to tell if we can trust them.

Sometimes it is difficult to trust immediately without sufficient and long-standing knowledge of and experience with the other. It seems silly to start an interpersonal relationship without first understanding the other person's trustworthiness and our ability to trust them. Trust often requires time to grow and develop. Moving too quickly in a personal relationship, before trust has been established, can put one into many difficult, life-changing events, all of which can negatively influence one's life. Putting love, sex, dependency, or commitment before one has fully developed trust in the other person can jeopardize one's future (Van Epp, 2007).

There are instances of mentally healthy-minded individuals who have initially been able to trust in the past but have learned that they can no longer trust others. Sometimes it is important not to trust someone. There are times when distrust is perfectly advisable and recommended, such as when asked to give out your bank information to a phone solicitor or in situations when you have an intuition or hunch, i.e., a healthy suspicion that a certain person is up to no good. Distrust does exist; not everyone is trustworthy.

---

[9] I won't be discussing the trust of objects here. For example, I trust that the yogurt that I am about to eat is safe and has not spoiled before the expiration date on the carton. I trust that my computer will turn on when I push the button. I will limit the discussion regarding trust only between people.

DISTRUST IN PARANOID INDIVIDUALS

The strength of a trusting relationship is not part of the life of paranoid people. They do not trust others and do not want people getting too close and personal with them; they dislike feeling vulnerable. If paranoid individuals are in an interpersonal relationship, they do not fully trust the person they are with. They rarely trust people and believe others are out to get them, deceive them, and cause them harm. Paranoid individuals believe they must, at all times, protect themselves from all other people—whether known to them or unknown. Erikson writes:

> In adults a radical impairment of basic trust and a prevalence of *basic mistrust* is expressed in a particular form of severe estrangement, which characterizes individuals who withdraw into themselves when at odds with themselves and with others (Erikson, 1968, p. 97).

They do not want others to get too close, to know them very well, or risk allowing others to find out what kind of person they are. They do not believe others will approve of them the way they are. They make it a priority to keep others out of their personal life.

Paranoid people do not want to accept what healthy-minded individuals know about honesty and trust; they only accept their own beliefs. Distrust may have little to do with the other person; paranoid individuals will not trust you. They resist trying to understand those around them. They may have a group of very honest and decent people around them, but they will still suspect others of being liars and cheaters about "everything." Not caring what it truly means to be honest, they only focus on their thoughts and beliefs of distrust. If what others say does not match their thoughts and beliefs, it confirms to them that everyone is dishonest and they must protect themselves.

As my discussion about Peter continues, he has become increasingly paranoid in the years to follow. He acknowledges that he is paranoid but does not understand why. He admits he has low self-esteem and believes mostly negative things about himself. He does not understand why he is so fearful of people and has thoughts that they are spying on him. In his words:

> *"I am afraid to go out in my yard. Neighbors always stare at me, and they think terrible things about me. I just know they think I'm stupid and strange. I don't trust them. I think of myself as weird, strange, and lazy too, but I don't like it when others think these things about me. I don't want to be hurt or judged by others. I am starting to worry about all these thoughts in my head, and I don't want others to know what I'm thinking. Am I going crazy?"*

From all outward appearances, Peter fits well as the typical adolescent, but he has stopped trying to do well in academics and sports because of his distrust for people and what they may think about him. He says he used to feel like "somebody." As was already mentioned, he was an outgoing child, involved in sports and his local church, but as he aged, he became more suspicious of people. Shortly before becoming an adolescent, Peter spent more time alone, afraid others would see him as "fake"—not a good person. He believed others judged him, and he did not like it. He does not trust people and asserts they are negatively judging him. In subsequent chapters, the connection between distrust and feeling judged will be spelled out further.

Paranoid people do not trust; they do not believe others are honest. They believe everyone is out to deceive them. What they believe has become their truth. If someone tries to prove to them that their thinking and beliefs are faulty, they will still believe that others are trying to deceive them. They will not let people get close to them, fearing others can read their minds and thoughts and worry they will be harmed in some way. They do not like being touched; they are very self-protective. Their trust boundary becomes reduced to a small distance, no one gets within this imagined boundary, and the paranoid person does not step out.

So, paranoid people do not trust *you* for what you say or do, even when they cannot see you. A healthy-minded individual might say that there is "proof" that someone cannot be trusted because of being betrayed in the past, but a paranoid individual does not need proof. Evidence will not convince a paranoid person that anyone is a trustworthy and caring individual. One can be honest at all times regarding all situations, and contrary to all logic and interpersonal truth, doubt and distrust will prevail in the paranoid mind. The longer a person has been paranoid, the more ingrained distrust of others has become. They question everyone's honesty; no one is honest, and no one is to be trusted.

JOEY

As another example, let me highlight the life of Joey, a 20-something young man who has struggled with paranoia for several years. He has not been diagnosed with schizophrenia, but it is possible he is going in that direction. Joey does not trust anyone well enough to spend any amount of quality time together. He is afraid to go outside his house because he knows someone is sitting up on the mountain with a rifle ready to shoot him. "I know I'm in their scope," he says.

Although he has never seen anyone sitting up on the mountain, and others have tried to "prove" to him that no one is there, he is convinced that someone is there. Joey continues,

"I don't trust people, and that's why I'm lonely. I prefer to be alone now. Even girls think I'm weird, so why should I go out there where people are?" Joey has no actual evidence that each person he encounters is distrustful, but he is very aware of what he believes, and he knows he does not trust people. He is fond of saying, "Trust is an illusion."

He has a couple of "acquaintances" whom he has known since childhood, but after a short while of visiting with them, he tells them they have to leave. "I don't trust them much, and I worry they might think there is something wrong with me. I don't want them to know me too well." Joey craves female companionship, mostly contained within his imagination, since he has not attempted to establish a relationship. He does not trust girls, fearing they will learn something about him that can be used as a weapon.

Joey's paranoia has been increasing for a few years, and he has been spending more time alone. Trust is almost non-existent to him. He trusts his mother "a little." He has developed a very low opinion of himself, often calling himself "weird" and "crazy." Joey uses his isolation to keep people at bay, to protect his privacy and insecurities. He sees a psychiatrist who has him on medication for anxiety and paranoia, but he does not trust this medication. "The doctor is trying to poison me, and I won't take his stupid medication. I don't need it; it does no good anyway." Joey does not enjoy talking to his therapist either. He worries about confidentiality and expects his therapist to "turn on me." After a brief attempt at therapy, Joey has decided he can think for himself and that he does not need any help from anyone.

Distrust is a significant aspect of the paranoid individual's life which is encountered in interpersonal relationships and with strangers—people at large. How does distrust in a few situations turn to distrust toward all humans? The paranoid person repeatedly tells themselves that no one is to be trusted. Since they are lonely, they have plenty of time to think about the broken trust of past experiences and the people around them. When they step outside in open view of others, they already do not trust them, those known or unknown to them, fearing what they might do or think about them.

They believe others are talking about them, conspiring against them, and that they may be physically harmed or have hateful, nasty remarks made about them. They distrust people so much now that they avoid being seen, allowing anyone to think their degrading and condescending thoughts. Deep and growing distrust confines them to live a lonely existence.

DELUSIONS

"If I can't trust them, why should I hang out with them?" says Joey. Even those who are "out there" but can't be seen and are unknown to him are suspect because the paranoid person *knows* they are there; all unseen and unknown others are suspect. In psychological terms, this is a delusion. Van den Berg has an insightful way of explaining delusion regarding a young man he was treating:

> He thinks, for instance, that a conspiracy has been set up against him. The healthy person notices nothing of this conspiracy, and he cannot prove to the sick person that he is mistaken. The mentally ill is unaffected by the evidence, no matter how convincing it may be and no matter how much it conforms to reality. One even gets the impression that the mentally ill wards off such evidence. The mentally ill will not accept the reality of the healthy. ...The way he relates to the conspiracy is real to him but not to us (van den Berg, 1972, p. 108).

Paranoid people believe in their delusions and live with them. They do not believe they will ever be able to trust another person. *No one* is trustworthy. Part of the difficulty of getting paranoid individuals to open up and talk about their paranoia is that they do not trust you. They keep their thoughts and feelings guarded so well that others may not even suspect paranoia. This is true in both personal and therapeutic relationships.

In therapy, the client will often keep their paranoia hidden behind anxiety, depression, and anger; they will not share their thoughts about what others are saying about them. They may remain silent about the perceived threats against them and their distrust of people. The therapeutic relationship requires trust as its foundation, which strongly counters these firmly-held beliefs of the paranoid client. If the client eventually trusts the therapist, then they may open up about their life and begin dealing with their paranoia. It may take the therapist a long time to build rapport, but this is required if they are to help this individual reconstruct their life and build relationships that are strengthened by honesty and trust.

MENTAL ILLNESS

Paranoia is a mental illness of varying degrees. While some readers may object to using the term *mental illness* when describing people, from a psychological perspective, mental illness is the falling short of general, overall mental health. Once one has achieved a certain level of understanding and has surpassed previous levels of mental illness, one can look back and understand better and more clearly what is meant by "mental illness."

Maslow described how one could only appreciate one's previous struggles when one has overcome one's limitations and "risen" to the next level. Only then can one see clearer what one has accomplished to overcome the "lower," more basic levels of need. Many forms of mental illness need not be permanent.

Paranoia can decrease if trust issues are confronted, dealt with, and integrated into the paranoid individual's personality. The trust constituent, one of the foundational supports of paranoia, can be strengthened, and one may then move closer toward mental health.

As we mature, our goal is to value a higher level of mental health and mental strength, a stronger personality, and greater achievement in all areas of life. It is not by ignoring one's mental health, by only occasionally working on one's weaknesses or emotional turmoil, that one achieves results. No, by repeated struggles and long, arduous work on one's weaknesses and challenges, one slowly sees results. Mental health is not a guarantee in life, it is an achievement, and one does not achieve mental health by reading and studying about it. It takes much work, patience, and practice.

SUMMARY

Paranoid people do not trust; they do not believe others are honest. They believe everyone is out to deceive them. What they believe has become their truth. If someone tries to prove to them that their thinking and beliefs are faulty, they will still believe that others are trying to deceive them. They will not let people get close to them, fearing others can read their minds and thoughts and worry they will be harmed in some way. They do not like being touched and are very self-protective. Their trust boundary becomes reduced to a small distance, no one gets within this imagined boundary, and the paranoid person does not step out. Let us now explore the paranoid individual's thoughts and emotions.

COGNITION AND
EMOTIONAL

P EOPLE OFTEN REFER TO PARANOIA as a "feeling" they get
when they believe they are being watched, or the unrelenting thoughts that others are talking about them behind their
back. However, as we have been exploring, paranoia is not just
a thought or feeling, but a developing lifestyle. Paranoia affects
the entire person: body, thinking, feelings, emotions, belief system, imagination, and social relationships. When one is paranoid, one *is* wholly immersed in all aspects of paranoia in the
way they are living-in-the-world. Even when they are not focusing on what others are saying about them, they are still paranoid because paranoia is a condition of living involving distrust,
loneliness, and low self-esteem.

Paranoid people actively participate in paranoia through
their manner of living. They believe others are watching, not only
people they can see, but people who are unknown to them. They
physically withdraw and shy away from people they believe can
harm them. Paranoid people are angry and fearful in their emotional expression toward the world. This chapter will examine the
emotional and cognitive aspects of the paranoid individual's life.
We will investigate the subjective experiences of paranoia to form

a more precise understanding of how paranoia lives in the individual's life. To better work with paranoid individuals in therapy, it is essential for the therapist to be cognizant of paranoia in its essence, in its everyday-lived-experience. The paranoid individual may then glean a better understanding of themselves before their paranoia becomes a chronic pathological condition.

Paranoia is not an experience that occurs outside of the realm of the emotionally-, mentally-, or physically-lived body. The paranoid person is wholly immersed in paranoia. Although they may not want to be paranoid, they live it, either temporarily, as situations in their life call them back to their vulnerabilities, or increasingly more permanent as paranoid experiences occur more often and become expected, i.e., part of one's personality. Probably the best place to reflect on how paranoia takes hold of the individual is at the beginning, before paranoia's growth and influence take over one's life.

ANXIETY

All paranoid people are anxious, but on the contrary, not all anxious people are paranoid. Anxiety is an *a priori* condition, a powerful prerequisite for paranoia's existence, but we must not confuse the two. Paranoia and anxiety are different experiences. It is as inconceivable to imagine paranoia existing without pre-existent anxiety as much as it is improbable to have a life that is free of anxiety. Just being human and living in the world is a source of anxiety, and the thought of permanently leaving this world (death) creates great anxiety for most people. Anxiety has far-reaching tentacles throughout human life experiences. We are born into anxiety, into an anxious world, and we struggle with it throughout much of our life. Heidegger says:

> In that in the face of which one has anx-
> iety...means as a phenomenon that *the*

*world as such is that in the face of which one
has anxiety*... What oppresses us is not this
or that...it is the world itself (Heidegger,
1962, p. 231).

Heidegger convincingly argues that anxiety is in this anxious world of ours, in our "everydayness" as we go about the projects of our lives, trying to understand ourselves and our anxious interactions with the world and the people in it.

I also appreciate the phenomenological work of William Fischer, who states:

Would it not be accurate to say that the
anxious experience is *the experience of being
impelled to actualize that for which my ability has already been apprehended as uncertain* (Fisher, 1988)?

By carefully studying this definition, we understand anxiety as an experience we feel forced to go through, but also our belief that we are not capable of getting through that experience successfully. Anxiety is feeling "forced" into experiences, moments in life when there is already the anticipation of not being able to do so, of not being able to succeed, and failure is inevitable. Anxiety anticipates failure and uncertainty. An anxious person says, "I can't do it, but I have no choice; I must do it even though I know I will fail."

Anxiety is often a life-expanding experience when we decide we must push ourselves through and learn about ourselves. The alternative would be to run from it. We cannot escape anxiety for the most part. We may not always feel anxious, but eventually, in life, we must come to terms with our deeper core identity and our inevitable death that always looms in the future. Anxiety informs us that we may be getting off track of our true nature.

Some people live with anxiety more outwardly expressed through physical and visible signs, e.g., nervousness, trembling, sweating, racing heartbeat, difficulty breathing, and avoiding life situations. Others try to ignore their anxiety, being ignorant of, covering over their symptoms through distraction, or with excessive altruistic, creative, or delinquent behavior. Others attempt to avoid anxiety through excessive chatter or by ongoing participation in risky behavior.

Anxiety existed *before* paranoia became part of one's life, and it may possibly exist as long as one has breath and looks forward, with apprehension and anticipation, to death. Anxiety does not magically or instantly disappear even if we take it seriously and deal with it moment to moment; it is a long-drawn-out process that requires time, patience, and in-depth personal study. Likewise, paranoia may not completely disappear as we work to understand it and how it has become integrated into our personality. Nevertheless, it is necessary to deal with paranoia alongside our other mental and emotional disturbances, and anxiety is the most powerful, ubiquitous, disturbing psychological influence.

As we have been discovering, anxiety already exists before the basic components of paranoia come into existence. Each paranoid person responds to the world in their own way and with their own understanding of what the world in general, and other people in particular, mean to them. They try to understand their paranoid way of relating to the world, how they react to fear and anger, and how they can, if they choose, learn to lower paranoia's influence before it negatively dominates their personality.

Anxiety is a great and powerful influence in life, and people often enter therapy to learn how to deal with this fact of life. Anxiety is the experience of fear that has become all-consuming but without a consciously known object of fear. The typical client does not care where anxiety comes from and its purpose; they just want the symptoms to go away.

A study in the British Journal of Psychiatry, whose aim was "To assess a wide range of paranoid thoughts multidimensionally and examine their distribution, to identify the associated coping strategies and to examine social-cognitive processes and paranoia" (Freeman, 2005), finds social anxiety to be, at least minimally, an experience of paranoia.

> We suggest that a lack of social self-confidence might make people feel vulnerable to attack and hence contribute to the occurrence of paranoia (Freeman, 2005).

A therapist may recognize social anxiety in a client if they are generally fearful in social situations and of being negatively evaluated by others. When the therapist asks a socially anxious person, "Why are you so anxious? What is it about people that frightens you so much?" they will often hear, "I don't know. It just happens," or they resort to a long, exhaustive dialogue of physical symptoms. But "I don't know" is probably the most correct answer a client can give regarding anxiety. When anxiety-ridden experiences occur, that person may not even know *why* anxiety exists or its purpose.

Anxiety is such a phenomenon that one most often does not consciously know all of what is contributing to it. Over the years, one may have forgotten when and how one's fears started in the first place, possibly being fearful from a very young age, and those original experiences of fear have long been forgotten or were prior to one's conscious knowledge.

One can consciously retain only a small amount of general knowledge at any one moment in life. One can ponder over memories, one's general fund of knowledge, facts, trivia, and current life problems, but other memories and vast sums of knowledge are inaccessible, "unconscious," separated from one's conscious mind due to the limited amount of knowledge that can be held consciously at the moment.

According to a theory of the mind, what one knows and is aware of is available to the "conscious" mind, while all other knowledge—suppressed, forgotten, or repressed—is moved to the "unconscious" mind. There is no actual division or line that separates these two "minds," and it is through closely observing our life that we appreciate what having a conscious and an unconscious mind means. I use the term "unconscious" to point to *what* I am not conscious of in the same way Jung would say:

> The concept of the *unconscious* is, for me, an *exclusively psychological* concept, and not a philosophical concept of a metaphysical nature. In my view the unconscious is a psychological borderline concept, which covers all psychic contents or processes that are not conscious, i.e., not related to the *ego* in any perceptible way. My justification for speaking of the existence of unconscious processes at all is derived simply and solely from experience, and in particular from psychopathological experience, where we have undoubted proof that... the ego knows nothing of the existence of numerous psychic complexes... (Jung, Psychological Types, 1971).

If I were to make a drawing of the two "minds" (Fig. A), the theoretical line that separates consciousness from unconsciousness is what I refer to as the "I don't know" line. I call it this because this is what most people say when asked why they are so anxious. "I don't know" separates what one consciously knows from what one doesn't know consciously. To know where one's anxiety actually points, we must get "beyond" the "I don't know."

Conscious Mind

I don't know

Unconscious Mind

Fig. A

One often does not know why they are anxious; they just know they have anxiety symptoms. Anxiety is an unconscious phenomenon and is well hidden from our conscious knowledge. If one investigates anxiety to its depth, one eventually discovers what has been hidden; one discovers their hidden fears and hidden truths. The source of anxiety is blocked from the conscious mind, but it is discoverable. This "I don't know" line separates the forgotten, yet-to-be-uncovered unconscious material from what one consciously knows, since the unconscious mind cannot be known directly. One learns that one can eventually uncover what has been hidden and reduce anxiety's negative power. Lurking behind the symptoms of anxiety is the likely birthplace of paranoia.

Fear

Paranoid people respond toward others in a distrustful, suspicious, and cautious manner; their outward expression is usually self-protective with either fear or anger. If we approach a paranoid person who is scared and suspicious, we witness a fearful response. If we approach a paranoid person who is suspicious and angry because they believe people pose a threat, we witness an angry response. First, let us examine fear and how it grows and complicates one's life while compounding paranoia. Then we will look at anger. The importance of looking at both fear and anger is that these emotions often have a counterbalancing effect, so if only one emotional expression is evident, we have to search for the other to understand the entire picture and connection these emotions have with paranoia.

In today's world, we are surrounded by fear, fear-mongering, threats, violence, and the various attempts society uses to deal with those fears. Natural fear is our recognition that something is harmful, that something threatens our life or wellbeing. When our life is in danger, fear rises and signals us to take action. If we only needed to deal with one situation of fear at a time, our fear would reduce once the situation is resolved. Fear can be predictable and anticipated, such as when watching a horror movie, or it can catch us off guard if we encounter, while taking a walk, an animal or snake that could harm us. We may often experience fear at the hands of other humans. DeBecker makes poignant remarks about how multiple forms of fear can take over one's life and begin dominating it. Multiple or constant fears can have debilitating effects on our life. Regarding fear, DeBecker states:

> We all know there are plenty of reasons to fear people from time to time. The question is, what are those times? Far too many people are walking around in a constant state of vigilance…
>
> Real fear is a signal intended to be very brief, a mere servant of intuition. But though few would argue that extended, unanswered fear is destructive, millions choose to stay there. They may have forgotten or never learned that fear is not an emotion like sadness or happiness, either of which might last a long while. It is not a state, like anxiety. True fear is a survival signal that sounds only in the

presence of danger, yet unwarranted fear
has assumed a power over us that it holds
over no other creature on earth (DeBecker,
1997, pp. 292-293).

Paranoia is not just another form of fear. It is not just others
watching us and scaring us. One can be observed all day while
sitting at work, in front of a classroom as a teacher, or lying on
the beach during vacation; that does not make one paranoid. Go
to a local mall, and there are probably cameras on the building
surveying the parking lot, so every action is observed, taped, and
stored as evidence just in case an infraction of the law occurs.

We are under surveillance where we work, when we walk
down streets in cities, and near buildings. Cameras point at us in
theaters, doctor offices, around homes and apartment complexes,
any place where heightened security is deemed needed. Do these
cameras keep us safe? Possibly, but they really only identify who
is in the direct line of the camera's sight. Again, all this does not
create paranoia. Otherwise, our entire cities would be paranoid.
Some people believe this is an invasion into the "personal" life,
knowing they are being spied upon. But what "personal" life are
they talking about: their appearance, make-up or sartorial flaws;
their way of walking; their habits; their thoughts?

Our lives are now more transparent than ever before with
the mass marketing campaigns of computers, the Internet, video
cameras, cyberspace, the "cloud," automatic collecting of personal data every time we log onto our computers or enter something into a search engine. Online searches and purchases are
tracked, and even grocery store purchases are tracked, so we are
offered coupons to influence future purchases. Why does it not
bother *everyone* that we are watched and spied upon? What about
the fear perpetrated through television and movies, the news
media, or expressed by parents to their children: "*Don't you know
there are kidnappers and pedophiles out there?*" We are told to be

on the lookout for terroristic threats and suspicious-looking persons. The world is a dangerous place, we are told unwaveringly.

Unfortunately, fear has become the predominant emotion of our time, not necessarily based on threats to our physical or psychological bodies, but more so on the *belief* that threats from known or unknown sources are impending and imminent. People fear someone will break into their home, so they keep the doors and windows locked at all times, curtains drawn tight, living in dark, gloomy rooms, worrying about who is outside spying on them.

Enormous sums of money are spent on monitoring and surveillance devices that are used to keep track of others. Lights automatically turn on if something comes too near the house. Cameras connected to computer monitors are now taping the movement of every animal or leaf that sails near the property of the fear-consumed consumer. Advertisers on TV push paranoid ideas to the extreme to sell the customers exactly what they "must have" to stay safe; "*You must have this burglar alarm, or you are not safe in your own home. You must be connected to our company so we can save your life by alerting the police when your home is invaded. You must protect your family…or maybe you just don't really care about them enough.*"

The paranoid mind starts to think that with the next bigger and more sophisticated camera, all worries will be over, for surely this will be the end of the misery and will reduce paranoia. Yet, as we will see in our ongoing discussion, surveillance cameras do not lower fears and worries related to paranoia.

That they draw the curtains tight doesn't really matter. The belief is that someone is still out there spying, threatening to invade at any moment. The threat of bodily harm is palpable when the paranoid person believes someone is "out there." Fear is powerful in a paranoid person; fear dominates that life. The paranoid person is fearful of being "observed" or "discovered" of his fears and deep secrets. The paranoid person lives his life in fear of being discovered, both by self-discovery and by others, of something too personal or possibly too self-damning. Paranoid people are not always consciously aware of these deep fears and personal secrets, but are impelled to protect them.

Paranoia is bound up with this great fear. The fear of being discovered or seen too intimately—by others and by self-discovery—requires the paranoid person to keep his personal life hidden, whether that which is hidden is true or not. What one thinks and believes about oneself and others may not be based on fact or reality, possibly having been believed for so long that it is no longer questioned for its truth.[10] One can believe wholeheartedly that no one loves them, but others do not believe that as truth and, in fact, may actually love them. One can hide and protect beliefs that are not true. Beliefs about oneself are protected from discovery by the consuming fear of being "found out." Fearing the magnifying glass peering into their depths, they worry about what others will see and what they believe themselves to be.

I wish to stress the point that what one believes and thinks about oneself may not be true, not be factual, but can be a distortion of reality, an irrational, inaccurate judgment of oneself. I use Freud's classic work on paranoia as an example and how he connected it to homosexuality. The belief that an unfulfilled homosexual wish is at the root of paranoia has long been debated but has not proven to be evident in this current study. What is significant are the underlying, often unrecognized, and unexpressed beliefs one has about oneself. He stated:

> Those whose case histories were examined
> by us were both men and women, of differ-
> ent races, professions and degrees of social
> standing, and we noted with surprise how
> clearly the defense against a homosexual
> wish was to be recognized at the core of the

---

[10] I refer the reader to *Social Cognition: How Individuals Construct Social Reality by* Rainer et al., or other reading material for a deeper understanding of cognitive bias.

pathological conflict in each of these cases and how all of them had come to grief in trying to overcome their unconsciously intensified homosexuality. This was not at all in line with our expectations. In paranoia, in particular, the sexual aetiology is in no sense obvious, with social humiliations and setbacks tending to be to the fore in its causation, especially in the case of men. We need only forge a little deeper, however, to recognize that the driving force in these social injuries is the part played by the homosexual components on the patient's emotional life. As long as normal activity prevents us from gaining insight into the depths of the life of the soul, we are inclined to doubt that the emotional relations between an individual and those around him in his social existence have anything to do with eroticism, in their factual character or their genesis (Freud, 1911/2003, pp. 50-51).

Freud referred to the unacknowledged and unexpressed homosexual wish that a person has repressed or suppressed, not wishing to acknowledge so as to keep his social standing. In this quote of Freud's, I find particularly interesting his acknowledgment that normal daily activity covers over and "prevents us from gaining insight into the depth of the life of the soul," in his case, the homosexual wish fulfillment, in our case, the actual roots of paranoia. I find no evidence that this is always a homosexual wish cover-up.

Paranoia is actually the avoidance of or denial of underlying thoughts, fears, and beliefs one attempts to keep secret. The paranoid person fears how other people may think and judge them. We can hear—if one really listens to one's self-talk—ourselves speaking to ourselves about our inadequacies and sensitivities, about our vulnerabilities and weaknesses. Paranoia helps us keep those thoughts and feelings at bay. We prevent ourselves from acknowledging these deep underlying torments, and we walk through life in fear of their discovery, both from ourselves and by others. But this fear of discovery may not be a repressed homosexual impulse. The paranoid individual hides their inner life from the outside world, and this inner life so scares and frightens them that they believe the worst of fate will happen if they are discovered. They protect themself, even from themself.

Paranoia's fear makes one want to run and hide from people. "I don't trust people enough to share my inner worries and beliefs. This is why I'm so lonely; I fear everyone," quoting Peter, whom I discussed in previous chapters. Peter admits he is afraid of people and would prefer to stay alone, even being afraid of going out with his friends. He says he does not want people to get to know him for fear they will be repulsed by what they find. Peter lives with the fear that he will be "uncovered" and "found out," discovered for his vulnerabilities and weaknesses. He keeps his sensitivities and vulnerabilities well hidden, well protected from prying eyes.

These hidden fears, vulnerabilities, sensitivities, and inadequacies may have nothing to do with sexual orientation. The overlying denial and avoidance of the unrecognized or unfulfilled secrets of the paranoid individual prevent them from recognizing and accepting these integral aspects of their nature, limiting and restricting themself from realizing who they are as an individual different from others. They protect what they think and believe about themself, even if these are *false beliefs*.

When Freud believed that the homosexual wish fulfillment was absolutely true in the paranoid individual—at the root of one's paranoia—he did not address the possibility that this individual *feared* this could be true, even if homosexuality never was true in action or desire for this individual. The paranoid person fears many of their self-beliefs and does not know if what they believe is, in fact, part of their genuine and authentic self, or part of their self-delusion. We now understand paranoia as the *avoidance* of unexpressed and unacknowledged self-beliefs of which one is sensitive and protective, and *fear* that others will snoop and examine these traits. If these beliefs do become exposed, the paranoid individual believes they will be ridiculed and humiliated.

ANGER

The paranoid person uses one of two ways, in general, to protect themself from being emotionally and vulnerably exposed to others; an outward expression of either fear or anger. We have just discussed how fear protects the paranoid individual from being exposed or "found out" and how they protect their inner feelings and beliefs from being spied upon by others. Now we shall delve into how anger is used to protect the paranoid person from the perceived disapproval they believe will come if others know who they "really are."

Anger is one's attempt to protect oneself from those who may intend to take advantage or do harm. One can use anger to defend oneself or to "draw a line in the sand" when others are too close—invading one's personal space—or a perceived threat and attack is imminent. Anger has much to do with feeling used, belittled, disrespected, or taken advantage of, not just once but over and over again. Anger is used to protest or protect oneself from a perceived or real invasion of one's freedom, the freedom to be who one is and to exist according to one's beliefs.

BOB

A slightly paranoid male social worker, Bob, is very good with and enjoys working with teenage boys in his therapeutic practice.

I use this example because of what I discussed in the previous few pages, that Freud identified a homosexual-wish fulfillment (the repressed or suppressed desire) as the root of paranoia, but as we have put forth, there are many deeper worries, fears, and feelings of vulnerability and sensitivities that bring paranoia to the surface, even if these deeper fears have much or little to do with sexuality. It is not the sexual sensitivity that "causes" paranoia, but the need to protect underlying sensitive beliefs and to avoid those deeply held beliefs that manifest in the individual.

Bob recounts the day a colleague remarked, "Bob likes teenage boys."

Bob immediately became angry; his paranoia reared up, and he said, "I've got a reputation to protect, and I don't want anyone f...ing with that reputation. I'll protect myself when I think someone is saying something negative about me or pointing at me, insinuating that I'm a pervert or child molester."

No matter what choice of words his unsuspecting colleague could have chosen, Bob heard that he was being accused of being a pervert, that he intimately likes boys and was capable of sexual impropriety with them. He felt compelled to correct that statement, and he needed to protect himself from anyone thinking or saying he was a pervert or molester. He was furious. After deeper emotional and cognitive reflection, Bob realized he was protecting his fear of being labeled as such. He was also trying to avoid a *self-imposed* identity by confronting, with an angry outburst, he who triggered that identity, and fleeing from this identity he does not want.

This inner identity is what Bob does not want others to know about, and he also does his best to hide this identity from himself. Bob has never shown a propensity toward perversion. He is a married man with children and has a talent for understanding and working with teenage boys, but he has deep-rooted fears he would be seen as a pervert. He does not want to be "found out," but what he hides from is not even true in reality and practice. He fears what he thinks. In fact and in objective truth, what he fears about himself is not even part of his being. Even though being a pervert has never been a reality for him and there has been no indication or exhibition that Bob ever was or ever will be a pervert, Bob admits that he thinks of himself as a pervert, but only in his thinking and private speech, never in action or manifestation. He fears the *beliefs* and *thoughts* he has about himself that are not even true.

Why does Bob think himself to be a pervert, and why does he feel the need to protect that untruth? This belief may have no basis in the reality of that person. Bob can think and believe anything he wants inside his head, even if it is not, in reality, true and correct. Kantor states:

> These delusions also take root in low self-esteem, that is, in a poor self-image, whether or not that poor self-image is warranted (Kantor, 2004, p. 28).

As I wrote earlier, low self-esteem is a component of paranoia, and negative self-esteem and self-image create thoughts, feelings, private speech, and beliefs based on that low self-esteem. Our interactions with healthy-minded individuals often make us aware of these beliefs, and we then have the opportunity to correct thoughts that border on delusional or "extreme." On being paranoid, truths and facts are not always the informer.

FEAR AND ANGER

Often the emotions of anger and fear become confused, one expressed in place of the other. Fear often wears the cloak of anger, and vice versa. Sometimes when one is angry, one only expresses their fear; likewise, when scared, one suppresses their fear and only shows anger. Let me use a common example that possibly everyone has experienced in some form:

If a toddler attempts to stick their finger into an electric plug socket, the parent may scream, "Get away from that," angrily jump up and perhaps slap the child's hand, threatening to punish the child if they try that again. What an angry expression! However, why is the parent angry? Could it be that the parent is actually scared for the child's safety?

The fear is kept inside, away from view, and the anger expressed is used to drive the point home that the parent is serious and does not want to see the child harmed. The anger may protect the parent from realizing their own fear of the quickness with which life can be snuffed out. Can you imagine the child's response if the parent shook with fear, cried, ran away, or fainted at the realization that their child could have been electrocuted? Not quite the same lesson will be taught to the child as with the outburst of anger.

In a contrasting example, a passive individual may be so shy and scared while out in public that instead of speaking up about a serious injustice, they hold in their anger and allow their fear to remain on the surface, effectively suppressing justified anger. Bullied children are often too scared or intimidated to speak up about how they are treated. They are more apt to keep their feelings to themselves, especially anger, and so we find that under the surface of fear is anger, potentially aching to get out. We protect the feelings and emotions that are more difficult for us to experience consciously.

EMBARRASSMENT

Embarrassment is a self-conscious feeling connecting quickly with fear and anger. One may avoid situations to avoid embarrassment. Embarrassment has the potential to injure one's sense of self, their self-esteem. One feels exposed, believing others can see into them, what they are hiding, what they feel, their inadequacies and vulnerabilities. The embarrassed person tries to protect their feelings from the scrutiny of others. Embarrassment is a kind of fear. It is one's attempt to hide one's inner thoughts, worries, low self-esteem, and feelings that have just been exposed through words or actions. As with fear, one has the option of fight, flight, or freezing in place. Alternatively, to suppress one's fear, one may lash out angrily at those in front of whom one has become embarrassed. The more difficult an emotion is to express, the easier it is to remain hidden.

Examining the contrast between anger and fear, sometimes, when one gets angry and has gotten angry so often about the same thing, they have forgotten what is at the core of his most common expressions of anger. Likewise, one can be anxious and fear living expressively, having lived this way for so long that they have forgotten what is at the core of their fears. Does one's fear prevent one from allowing anger to surface? Does one's anger prevent one from allowing fear to surface?

I use an ordinary coin as a metaphor to demonstrate the reciprocity of fear and anger, the contrast and similarity of these two emotions. I keep a coin in my desk at work—just an ordinary quarter—but I tell the younger children and teens that this coin can tell us things that they may not realize about themselves. They are usually intrigued. This works well with elementary-age children and adolescents who have been getting in trouble with their anger or hiding behind their fears and do not understand how to handle their emotions. I have also found it helps adults formulate and identify the feelings and emotions they express freely and also the emotions that struggle to come to the surface.

CINDY

A ten-year-old girl, Cindy, recently came to my office because she was getting in trouble for fighting at home and school. She has difficulty getting along with others. I showed Cindy this coin and explained to her that the "heads" side of the coin is what I shall call *the anger side*, and when I turned the coin over, this is what I will call *the fear side*. Fear and anger are very difficult to experience outwardly at the same time; usually, only one emotion at a time sees the light of day, but we know that the other emotion is somewhere close by.[11]

Since we can only see one side of the coin at a time, I explained to Cindy that if she is angry all the time and her outward expression is anger, what we cannot see is the hidden side, the fear. She connected readily with this while I showed her the "heads" side of the coin and talked about how her anger easily shows up on the surface. Then I asked her, "So where do you think the fear lives?"

Cindy understood where this was leading and said, "I keep that on the inside."[12]

I talked with Cindy about how she keeps some emotions hidden, and the importance of discussing these unexpressed emotions. It is beneficial to talk about buried emotions, and we can make great strides in therapy when dealing with what our client keeps "hidden" and out of view. Outwardly expressed fear or anger often hold the other emotion in abeyance, but both are required for a healthy balance.

Paranoid people exhibit either anger or fear outwardly, and we know they hold in the other emotion—either through repression or by conscious suppression—keeping it hidden from the world. If a paranoid person is angry as their outward expression, they tend to suppress their fears and will only show them if sufficient trust has been built. This "hiding of emotions" may

---

[11] If the child is anxious, nervous, and is experiencing a lot of fear about her life, I point to the "head's" side of the coin and call that *the fearful side,* and then I point to the "tails" side and call this *the angry side.* If anger is heads, fear is tails. If fear is heads, anger is tails.

[12] And the reverse is true as well. If Cindy is expressing fear outwardly, she usually keeps the anger hidden. I then ask her where she must be keeping her anger since others around her can't see it. She responds with "Inside" or "In here," pointing to her chest or stomach.

have resulted from a lifelong inability of this person to allow one emotion, the fear *or* anger, from being appropriately expressed at the appropriate time. Usually, only anger *or* fear is outwardly expressed in paranoia; the other is kept hidden.

THINKING

As is true with most psychological problems, paranoia takes over and affects one's entire life, incorporating the past and affecting future decisions and relationships. One thinks in a paranoid manner, believes others are talking about them, or "are out to get me," and this is felt subjectively as fear or anger. Therapists also benefit by understanding the thinking process of paranoia, how it differs from non-paranoid thinking, and how loneliness, distrust, and low self-esteem negatively affect this individual's thinking.

How is one's thinking influenced, altered, and changed by paranoia, and how does one's thinking contribute to paranoia? A substantial part of a paranoid person's experience is a rigid thinking process.

People who are paranoid do not take responsibility for their thinking. They believe that whatever they think is the truth and everything they say is the truth. There is an inner conflict between opposing thoughts and beliefs, which is experienced as an external conflict between oneself and others.

> In such ways, the intensification of internal conflict gives rise to an intensification of defensive sensitivity to external figures. The process we call projection goes farther than such defensive sensitivity but is a product of it. When internal tension intensifies defensive tension, the defensive mobilization becomes more rigid. Sensitivities become

more acute, more anticipatory, and more
rigidly biased in their anticipations. The
individual is no longer merely sensitive to
the possibility of a slight, for example, but
expects it and looks for it, even obsessively
(Shapiro, 1981, pp. 141-142).

Paranoid thinking is negative and degrading self-scrutiny.
It is usually negative, judgmental, rigid, and harsh thinking,
identifying and focusing on areas of one's own personality and
belief system that are psychologically weak and perceived as
inferior. However, the individual may not be consciously aware
that they are doing this. The paranoid individual is suspicious
in the same way that they think most negatively about themself.
They listen to their delusional, self-deceptive thoughts and may
have had no one help them correct that thinking.

Remember, paranoid people feel alone and usually do not
share their thoughts with anyone, so a delusional thought continues growing and becomes harder to change once it sets root.
Just to reiterate a previous important point, these thoughts are
not hallucinations. They are, in fact, one's own thought processes that sound like an inner voice covertly using negative and
suspicious judgment. The paranoid person has given their life
over to this delusional thinking and self-deception.

In the beginning stages of developing paranoia, one may be
successful at "putting aside" their paranoia for a while through
distraction or reasoning. They can change their loneliness by
associating with others and possibly feel better. The negative
self-judgment and deprecating feeling-tone may be objectified
or ignored. They can risk trusting others and realize some people are trustworthy. Kantor remarks:

Some paranoid individuals retain *a modest
degree of insight* into themselves. As such,
to at least some extent, they seem to know

91

that they are troubled. Many of them take
the next step and try to keep quiet about
their paranoia, which they therefore only
manifest in the subtlest of ways (Kantor,
2004, p. 12).

But why does paranoia grow in some people's lives more
than others? Why do some increasingly develop it to an extreme,
taking on pathological proportions? If one's loneliness and isolation, distrust, and low self-esteem are not acknowledged and
reduced, paranoia can grow as the years grow.

But even those who retain the ability to
recognize their paranoia often lose sight of
its extent. They recognize that sometimes
their thoughts and feelings are inappropri-
ate, that they make too much of unimportant matters, and that they are occasionally
hypersensitive, unnecessarily retaliative,
and even unrealistic, but they do not recognize the degree to which they are troubled (Kantor, 2004, p. 13).

So, what happens if one ignores the signs of increasing
paranoia for too long, or if they convince themself that they
are not paranoid, believing that other people really are talking
about them and really are out to get them? They are still paranoid. Thoughts and feelings do not create paranoia but are
expressed in paranoid ways according to the degree to which
paranoia has taken over their life.

As young children are active with egocentric speech—the
self-centered talk that is not being addressed to anyone in particular—they talk to themselves and explore various aspects of
their emerging world. When they play with their toys or with
other children, they may speak about their imagined situations

in their present life, and how they imagine themselves when older. If one listens closely, one can hear how children understand and deal with their life, their struggles with stress, confusion, or difficult situations related to interactions with their parents or their limited social life.

As examples of this kind of talk, I recently overheard a little boy, while playing with several trucks and farm toys, say, "This is *your* job, buddy, but I'll help you if you want," and while a little girl was playing with a few dolls, creating a little circle of her "make-believe" real friends, she said, "Sally really doesn't like us anymore. She has her own friends." Egocentric speech is frequently spoken aloud until about the age of 6–7 years, eventually turning inward—earlier if adults too often call attention to it and embarrass the child for talking to themself. This self-talk does not stop, but to the great sadness and bewilderment of interested and caring parents, the outwardly expressed self-talk becomes quiet, turns inward, and is then referred to as *private speech.*

A child's thinking is now reflected in their private speech, and adults are no longer privileged to know and hear what the child is thinking. This private speech is the internalized personal thoughts and reflections upon experiences of the child's life: school, themselves, friends, parents, strangers, and the future. It is also the talk they use to explain their feelings and emotions to themself. The child's private speech is intertwined now with their self-judgment, which includes a compilation of and reflection upon what others have said about them.

If a child is lonely before their private speech goes inward, there may be attempts to self-support and self-soothe their feelings; as Cindy, the little girl from above, later remarked, "I think they like me. I'll try to make friends with them tomorrow." Loneliness by itself in childhood does not cause paranoia, but as we continue to realize, loneliness contributes to silence, introversion, and self-analysis that may not be healthy, true, or factual. In some cases, one's private speech can be used to denigrate oneself; for example, when the child exclaims, "What's wrong with me? Why don't no one like me?"

Once their self-talk turns inward and becomes private, parents will have difficulty helping their child address loneliness and feelings. The influential adult will have to interact lovingly more often with the child to assist with their emotional struggles. If a child were to share their thoughts with a sympathetic and caring adult, much of the negative self-judgment and self-esteem issues could be addressed early, possibly holding off years of negative self-opinion and negative private speech. But the lonely child has no one else to talk to but themself, alone now with their private speech, no outside opinion counts, and no other opinion is entered into their conversation.

Sullivan addresses this time in a child's life as the possibility of loneliness taking hold and affecting his future. He writes:

> In a good many instances, circumstances do not permit very much of this audience behavior of the authority figures, and the child is actually lonely; and loneliness at this stage is a foreshadowing of the loneliness which we will be discussing later. The 'lonely' child, the child who cannot obtain the presence and participation, however passive, of elder folk, inevitably has a very rich fantasy life— that is, he makes up for the real deficiencies by multiplying the so-called imaginary personifications which fill his mind and influence his behavior (Sullivan, 1953, p. 223).

How do any of us know what a child is thinking? A lonely child keeps their thoughts and feelings to themself, and if no one questions them or encourages them to express themself, then their private speech and feelings remain isolated and quiet, i.e., introverted. A child who does not talk about their thoughts and feelings isn't allowing their thoughts to be examined by a "friend" or concerned adult. Can we say for certain that their thoughts, beliefs, and self-opinions are always correct and justifiable? The child's fantasy life increases with no ability to self-measure its truth. According to Sullivan, this can become a source of trouble in the child's life, stating:

> Here is another of these rather circular processes, approximating a vicious circle: already the child has had to develop a rich fantasy life to make up for the lack of audience and of participation by the authority figures, and from this lack the child is apt to be relatively undeveloped in the very quick discrimination of what is his private fantasy and what may be consensually validated; that in turn exposes the juvenile to ridicule, punishment, and what not, and so tends to give the feeling of risk in life (Sullivan, 1953, p. 225).

INTRALOCUTION

A child can think anything about themself even if it is not based on fact or truth, but if it is not spoken aloud, it can cement into a belief that forms a core of negative self-judgment. I refer to this inner speech, self-talk, and private speech as *intralocution*, how one speaks to oneself within the brain's closed network system. Intralocution is the inner conversation one has "inside one's own head," of which one can think and believe whatever one wants, in private, with no justification to its truth, and this can plant the seed for delusion. It differs from *inter*locution in that it does not involve another person but is a conversation one has with oneself, all by oneself.

Intralocution is best examined aloud with a healthy-minded adult of strong psychological character who understands childhood development and has an interest in and compassion for children. Consciousness is fragile in a child at this age, and what is planted becomes viable, whether it is good or bad for one's personality.

During the next development phase, preadolescence, meaningful peer relationships, and increased social situations are essential prerequisites for health and psychological development, as Sullivan clearly states:

> Because of the rapidly developing capacity to revise one's personifications of another person on the basis of great interest in observation and analysis of one's experience with him, it comes about that the preadolescent phase of personality development can have and often does have very great inherent psychotherapeutic possibilities. ...Because one draws so close to another, because one is newly capable of seeing oneself through the other's eyes, the preadolescent phase of personality development is especially significant in correcting autistic, fantastic ideas about oneself or others. I would like to stress...that development of this phase of personality is of incredible importance in saving a good many rather seriously handicapped people from otherwise inevitable serious mental disorder (Sullivan, 1953, pp. 247-248).[13]

---

[13] Be careful not to confuse the meaning of autistic from the time when Sullivan wrote this, to the meaning of "autism" as it is commonly used today.

Even the reverse receives much research support; poor relationships contribute to poor adjustments and depression, and a struggle through adolescence development. If the pre-adolescent is lonely, isolated, and has no one to talk to, that child starts to think of themselves as a problem; "Something must be wrong with me," they believe. Their intralocution is more negatively self-directed.

During Erikson's fourth stage of developmental conflict—Industry vs. Inferiority—just before the onset of adolescence, the pre-adolescent is tested for his ability to "make it in the world" with confidence, and for his ability to handle life confidently. As Muuse describes Erikson's work:

> If a child fails in the task to acquire a feeling of success and a desire for recognition for work well done, there will be a lack of industriousness and a feeling of usefulness. Such children may not develop the feeling of enjoyment and of pride for good work. On the contrary, they may be plagued by feelings of inadequacy and inferiority and may become convinced that they will never amount to much. As a result, there is *work paralysis* and a *sense of futility* that will most likely contribute to ego diffusion in the next stage (Muuss, 1996, p. 51).

Now, let us discuss the adolescent stage of development, twixt twelve and twenty, when the developing child's social life or lack thereof greatly affects how the teenager thinks and perceives themself. The teen's thinking often becomes deeply personal and imprisoned unless they allow for a continuous expression of those thoughts and feelings and feel confident to do so. As the teen grows, their thoughts may remain closed, introverted, and stifled, but as we have discussed before, this does not automatically produce paranoia.

The teen may not be lonely, have low self-esteem, or feel overly judged by others, but this age group tends to feel overly judged and evaluated by peers. The imaginary audience of adolescence theory states that teens believe they are being watched and judged by those around them. When one's body is being observed, they believe others know what they are thinking; they anticipate what others are thinking about them, and they feel judged. This judgment can be positive or negative, supportive or harsh, depending on their self-esteem.

If the teen is lonely, what do they do with thoughts of being negatively judged by others? The lonely adolescent stays quiet and is subjected to their intralocution, which may have turned very negative depending on their developed self-esteem. Extroverted teens may have less trouble expressing their thoughts and opinions about how others judge them than their introverted cohorts, hence being able to maintain positive social support. Nevertheless, extroverted teens are not protected from the development of paranoia outright. If their intralocution is self-disdainful, or a developing narcissistic personality believes that others' judgments put them higher and more prominent than their social counterparts, then their experiences of loneliness have more to do with grandiosity.[14]

Adolescents' thoughts are personal, and no one else is privileged to know their thoughts if they are unwilling to share them. They often think and interpret what they believe without input from others. If their intralocution does not truly reflect facts that can be verified, they can become delusional.

---

[14] Paranoid individuals are known to fluctuate between paranoia and narcissism possibly due to the bi-poles in extremes of self-esteem. An inflated ego and exaggerated grandiosity promotes narcissism, while a deflated ego and low self-esteem promotes paranoia. Being narcissistic can be a very lonely experience. The inflated or deflated ego has much to do with self-esteem and vice versa.

Remember, one can think and believe anything one wants about this world, about anyone or anything—and we all have the right to do that—even if those thoughts or beliefs are not correct or acceptable to others. Intralocution without others' objective involvement can lead to all sorts of delusions and incorrect assumptions. Developing one's beliefs and thoughts about the world to the exclusion of others promotes rigid and purely subjective bias, and Shapiro concerns himself with this when he writes:

> In short, such an attitude guarantees the polarity between the self and the external world. Lacking it, one can find evidence to substantiate any bias; unknowingly, an objective relationship with the world is replaced by egocentricity and subjectivity. Thus, the rigid bias of defensiveness leads to the repeated "discovery" of the unrecognized products of its own concerns and preoccupations (Shapiro, 1981, p. 170).

One's intralocution needs outside influence to move towards creative and healthy outlets, without which a rigid and delusional direction is more likely.

JAMIE

Let me give you an example of something believed by a teenage girl who told me it was passed on to her by her mother. Jamie has a growing propensity toward paranoia and finds it very difficult to be around other people. She hates going outside her house where others can see her. She believes others are saying things about her and plotting to attack her. During a counseling session, she said her right ear was hot, and she believed this meant that someone was saying bad things about her.

I asked her to explain that, and she stated that if her right ear was hot, it meant someone was saying bad things about her, but if it was her left ear that was hot, it meant someone was saying nice things about her. How did Jamie come to believe this? This is an example of a superstition and family delusion, which has now become her personal delusion.

When questioned about how often her right ear burns, she says, "All the time." I then asked how often she hears things about herself that are positive, and she said, "Oh, I don't hear any of that." Jamie believes this and says it is always true, that she can hear people talking about her even though no one is around, and that is all the proof she needs to confirm that others, seen or unseen, are saying negative things about her.

Paranoid individuals are not the only ones to believe superstitions and family delusions passed to them and accepted as truth. Superstitions are rampant, and one can believe many things that are eventually proven not to be factual—like make-believe, gossip, or incomplete information—and without the input of a trusted other, society at large, or scientific facts as supplied to us through research, one cannot be sure if one's thinking is always correct and factual. If I believe someone else is negatively talking about me and interpret these negative statements as truth, then I believe it is a fact. I may then think of myself in this negative way, especially if it is repeated over and over in my intralocution.

If I am lonely and have no one else around me to bounce my thoughts and beliefs off, there will be little opportunity for self-correction, and my intralocution is now wrapping itself around itself without redress. The seeds of paranoia are being planted. Although negative thinking alone does not necessarily lead to paranoia, one's intralocution maintains the negative inner conversation, becoming negatively self-judgmental and feeding negative self-esteem.

The thinking of a paranoid person is narrow, rigid, and judgmental. They judge themself negatively. This could have its roots early in life through unchecked and unshared thinking. Paranoid thinking believes that others are out to get them, threatening them and putting them down, calling them names, and ridiculing them. They believe they are under the watchful and controlling eye of others. Following Shapiro's words:

> In paranoid conditions, rigidity is much more severe, and so is the loss of objectification. The defensive mobilization of will against external threat introduces the most rigid and restrictive kind of bias into the paranoid individual's attitude toward the world. To put the matter simply, open-mindedness is a luxury that those who feel vulnerable cannot afford. ...The person who feels vulnerable in this way must respect anything that suggests the possibility of personal threat, however remote, and must distrust anything that appears to be innocuous (Shapiro, 1981, p. 168).

The paranoid person generally does not want to understand themself—to be "open-minded"—that self-discovery will be too great, too fearful. They would rather live with blinders so they cannot see into the scary and threatening world, keeping others out, even if the other is capable of helping with mental and emotional stability. The fear of another person knowing the paranoid individual becomes so great that it promotes isolation and distrust to protect oneself. The paranoid person does not think highly of themself, and they are afraid others will also discover their negative self-evaluation and self-judgment.

FEAR AND PARANOIA

Paranoia describes a fearful life: mind, body, and emotions. It infiltrates relationships and often creates havoc. These people experience others as a threat, whether that threat is real or imagined. Before concluding this chapter on the cognitive and emotional relationship with paranoia, it is imperative to understand the difference between paranoia and the emotion of *fear*. Fear is defined as "a distressing emotion aroused by impending danger, evil, pain, etc., whether the threat is real or imagined; the feeling or condition of being afraid."[15]

When a non-paranoid person has an encounter with another person or a perceived threat, and that threat calls forth danger for potential harm, fear can be the life-saving instinctual reaction, and one will react to his fear in his usual manner: fight, flight, or freezing in place and doing nothing. If the paranoid individual believes someone or something is about to do them harm or is threatening to meddle in their personal life, they will experience fear. But what if this threat is not or never was an actual physical threat, an actual someone originating this potential for harm?

The paranoid individual believes there is a threat when, from a non-paranoid view, there is none. Paranoia is not wholly an experience of fear, but an experience with the "other," seen or unseen, whom one perceives as a threat. Distrust, low self-esteem, and the belief that others are threatening bring fear to the paranoid person, but an objective observer sees no outward threat. Paranoia is an encounter of fear, but it is more of an encounter with a *belief*—a belief that an "unknown other" is watching, observing, calling names, belittling, threatening, mocking, or spying.

---

[15] "Fear," Dictionary.com (Dictionary.com), accessed November 5, 2022, http://www.dictionary.com/.

This "other" may be an observable person but may also be "unknown," someone "out there" who remains hidden in the shadows, just beyond view, but who is perceived as dangerous, threatening, and suspiciously interested in the paranoid individual's personal life. This "unknown other" is the threat that is experienced as paranoia. Here I will introduce the term *"unknown-other"* as a description of someone believed to be "out there," who is not necessarily seen, but who watches and observes one's behavior, and who can be "felt" to be there.

It is important to distinguish between the unknown-other—which is a perceived fear of paranoid thinking—and a real, living, 3-D physical body standing in front of you, which could be threatening and has the potential for a real attack—which is not paranoia, but an actual experience of fear. The unknown-other is not an actual "somebody" who is watching and acknowledging the existence of the paranoid person. Fear is the predominant emotion at this time, the belief that the threat from the unknown-other is impending and imminent, but no physical attack occurs. The paranoid person cannot always look out yonder and see who the observer is, if there is an actual person out there, but it is unimportant and inconsequential if no observing other can be seen. Paranoid thinking tells them there is someone out there watching, observing, scrutinizing, and judging, but the unknown-other is not where they are looking. The unknown-other is self-based, subjective, or, in psychodynamic terms, a projection.

There is a strong sense of needed protection to keep the unknown-other from witnessing and spying on the self-perceived weakness and inferiority of the paranoid person. They worry that the unknown-other will discover their weakness, self-condemnation, and negative self-scrutiny. The object of their fear, the unknown-other, is not yonder, there, in the world. Since the unknown-other is subjective only, this strengthens and confirms paranoia, not as an encounter with another person, but an encounter with oneself—one's intralocution—experienced as fear.

Summary

The psychological twist that gives paranoia its power over the individual is that the object of this fear, the unknown-other, is not out there in the world, but is self-based. Paranoia is not an encounter with another, but an encounter with oneself. Another way of saying this is that the unknown-other is a metaphor for fear, harsh judgments, negative self-scrutinizing, threats to one's self-esteem, and one's sense of vulnerability. The unknown-other is not immediately *consciously* realized, but it is pervasive. It is one's actual intralocution that mocks and scrutinizes oneself and matches one's own negative self-evaluation. The harsh judgment, distrust, and self-scrutiny are an active part of the paranoid person's everyday lived-experience, even if not consciously realized.

Paranoia lays open the *fear* that one is ridiculed, belittled, or embarrassed by others, but this ridicule, belittling, and embarrassment is often not consciously realized—one's intralocution—but is believed to be that of the unknown-other. The paranoid individual is afraid to share their thoughts and feelings. They keep them well hidden, and we, from the outside, are not privileged to know what they are thinking. Acknowledgment of one's intralocution leads to a deeper understanding of what paranoia means to one's life. The experience with the unknown-other will be dealt with in greater detail in the next chapter.

THE UNKNOWN-OTHER

ONE OF THE FIRST WAYS we may come to realize a person is paranoid is when they tell us they are very suspicious of other people, that others are talking about them in very degrading ways, or when they believe others are out to harm them. Paranoid people suspect others are talking about them and observing them, as if they are on stage under a spotlight, the center of everyone's attention. They "feel" others' eyes upon them and just know they are being referred to in derogatory and mean-spirited ways.

A particular aspect of paranoia is believing they can actually and accurately hear what others are thinking and saying, even when the suspected observer is nowhere in sight. They believe others are saying negative and belittling things, that their intralocution is the voiced words of these "others." Paranoia dominates and becomes so ingrained that one gradually accepts paranoia as truth without really knowing what it is or why it is there. The paranoid person believes that when others are hatefully talking about them, eventually, this will turn into additional others doing the same thing, thus leading to more planning and plotting against them.

EXAMPLES OF PARANOIA: KEVIN

Let me give examples by using common experiences of paranoia. Here is how a hospital patient, Kevin, described his paranoia which has increased since he was young. He prefaces his story by saying this occurs at home, in a store, at church, or practically anywhere, whether or not he can see others around.

"When I leave my house, I immediately think the neighbors are all at their windows staring at me, mocking me for who I am and what I am doing. This has happened to me since I was young, but I never really thought so much about why it was happening. At some point, before I became an adult, I became concerned about why others were so interested in me and why they spent so much time at their windows. Was there something about me that interested them so much? Didn't they have anything better to do? When I go outside of my house, I can feel their eyes on me. I hear them criticizing me. They say things like, 'He's so stupid. He thinks he's great, but he ain't shit. He has no friends; no one likes him.'

"I feel like going back in the house so I can't be seen, and they won't be able to talk about me. Since I've gotten older, I logically know those people aren't standing at their windows. I cannot see them when I look, but I can still feel their eyes on me and hear what they are saying about me. They know things about me they can't possibly know. Do they have to be so mean? They call me names and try to make me feel bad, and I wonder if I can do anything right. They make fun of me. They dig at me where I am most sensitive. I want to hide from them. I can't get them to shut up. I get angry just talking about this."

This is not an unusual experience when a paranoid person goes out in public. For Kevin, when he is out in open spaces, he believes he is the center of others' attention and that he hears what they are saying about him. He believes he cannot do anything right and is being judged harshly for being himself. As Kevin tells it, these observing others seem to know quite a bit about him. They are very cruel towards him, using harsh words and digging judgments. "Who are these people? Why are they so interested in me, and how do they know so much?" is the question of the paranoid person. Kevin says he now pays *more* attention to the voice of these others than he does to what he is doing at the moment. This unknown other, he thinks, wants to take over and control his life.

In an earlier chapter, I discussed the lonely and isolating aspects of paranoia and how loneliness and isolation give one plenty of time to think and ponder about oneself and others. How is it that the lonely paranoid individual hears what others are saying about him, even though the other—seen or unseen—is out of range of hearing, or no one is actually around to speak? Who is saying these things, and why are their words so personal and negatively judgmental?

Paranoid thinking believes that someone is out there watching, observing one's every movement as if under a magnifying glass. All of one's actions are identified and magnified in great detail. As one paranoid client stated, even when she is alone in her home with the curtains tightly drawn, "Down deep inside, I have the overwhelming feeling that someone is outside looking in." Most of the time, there is no one in sight, but she just *knows* someone is watching her and talking about her.

Paranoia is a distraction from one's activities, projects, work, and peace of mind. This voice that the paranoid individual is listening to has an "authority" to it. It speaks as if it knows everything about the paranoid person: their depths, weaknesses, fears, sensitivities, imperfections, and vulnerabilities. This voice forces itself and is often unrelenting.

CONNER

Conner believes someone is always watching him. He does not see anyone when he is alone in his room, but he can "feel" them.

Conner spends most of his time alone, playing with his toys or on his computer. He is socially awkward and does not get along with others very well, often referring to himself as "weird." He is careful with how he behaves so he does not get into trouble at home and school. Especially when he is alone in his room, Conner is afraid that whoever is watching him will not approve of what he is doing; he believes this person does not like him or approve of his behavior. He looks around, but he does not see anyone there. He lives in fearful anticipation of someone discovering that he fears being seen. He imagines someone floating above him, observing him. Is Conner experiencing what Edinger calls the basis of paranoia, the observing "Eye of God"? Edinger states that in the paranoid experience, one's ego:

> ...projects the Eye of God into the environment so that the ego has the experience of being watched, listened to, and persecuted (Edinger, 1995, p. 67).

Is Conner "projecting" onto his surroundings his fears of being seen, and possibly exposing who he is? Does he believe he is under the ever-watchful and omnipresent eye of "God," the eye watching his ego? At 14 years of age, Conner says these experiences have been slowly coming on for years. He believes his parents watch him and know everything he does. He is afraid of making a mistake. Does he "feel" the eyes of his ever-watchful parents hovering above?

Conner believes his parents always know when he has done something wrong. He believes no one listens to him or cares about him and that whoever is watching him calls him a "lazy moron" and an "idiot." The voice tells him he is a stupid, intellectually deficient kid. He often hears, "You are a terrible person," coming from it.

For years Conner has tried to prove to others that he is not the bad kid they all think he is but he admits he just cannot seem to do his best. He believes kids think he is weird, crazy, and odd, and whenever he is out in public, he believes people notice what a weird and crazy kid he is. He makes little audible noises to drown out the judgmental and unsatisfied voice in his head, the one that disapproves of him the way he is. He states he wishes he was someone else so he could then be himself. Does that make sense? He wants to be someone else, so the disapproving voice in his head will finally be able to approve of him as someone acceptable; maybe then he could feel like himself and be happy with himself being himself.

Conner has all the basic and constituent influences for paranoia. He spends much time alone, has a low self-image and self-esteem, and trusts no one, including his parents. He thinks others are always talking about him to the point he believes what they say, and he catches himself using the same negative and hurtful words towards himself. When he tries to ignore the voice that calls him a moron, he cannot because he calls himself a moron. His odd and peculiar ways do not give him the confidence to fit into the world around him.

Since everyone is suspect to a paranoid person, I refer to this "other," the one who is out there watching and observing, as the "*unknown-other.*" This unknown-other knows where you are at all moments, can see all your actions, and anticipates your next move before you make it. "They see every movement I make, everything I do," one client stressed. Paranoid people feel they are under a magnifying class, but it is the unknown-other who sees into their depths, knows their feelings, thoughts, and the worst of their fantasies and imagination. The unknown-other is there when you are alone in the house and in public. The unknown-other knows what you think, knows your habits, your feelings, and is judging you for who you are and even for whom you are not. You are the center of attention from the unknown-other, being scrutinized, mocked, observed, and otherwise opened up for inspection.

The paranoid person believes they can hear the voice of the unknown-other in their head, and since what the unknown-other says is so personal, they fear that everyone else also knows these personal things about them. They become increasingly afraid of what *else* people might think of them. They fear being around others. They withdraw, isolate themself, and try to avoid contact with others. Fearing others are getting to know them and getting too deeply involved in their life, they further withdraw from people.

They fear the unknown-other and what it says about them. "In fact," one client stated, "I think about myself in the same way, but I do not want others to know me that well. I must protect myself from letting anyone know me any better, especially my dark and embarrassing thoughts. I protect myself by staying away from them, away from their eyes that stare at me and try to figure me out. I must protect my privacy. I must protect my personal life from them." The downward spiral into paranoia continues, and they start believing paranoia may be permanent; that is, there may be no escape from it.

The paranoid person suspects not only the unknown-other but also others they know and see daily. The paranoid person thinks like this: "Does the boss think bad things about me? Do my friends know my deep, dark thoughts? How many people are keeping their beliefs and feelings about me secret; do others think these bad and terrible things about me? Who can I trust? If the person whom I work alongside is really thinking I'm a pervert, how am I supposed to 'be myself' around them? Now I can't even trust those around me whom I used to trust. I have to distance myself and be more suspicious of them. I must keep my guard up at all times. Why don't they just mind their own business and keep their thoughts to themselves?"

Being around others is very difficult because of trust issues, and the paranoid person excludes more and more people whom they suspect and don't trust. They may eventually exclude everyone, all people on the planet, including those they have met in the past. No one is to be trusted. Everyone is out to get them. From Shapiro, we learn:

> From this standpoint, in other words, the projective identification of the enemy in the shadows can be seen as the product of a nervous, defensively searching and anticipating—suspicious—attention. Once the paranoid person has identified the threat, there is a further mobilization—in intensification of guardedness, suspiciousness, defensive antagonism—against it (Shapiro, 1981, p. 137).

The voice of the unknown-other speaks to the paranoid person. You may not see them, but you know they are always there. A paranoid client states, "I went out into the front yard to do some yard work, and I just knew the neighbor from across the road was staring at me. I looked over and couldn't see anyone; then I remembered my neighbor had moved in the past week, so no one could be in the house. But my thoughts told me someone must have broken into the house overnight, and that's who was now staring at me because I knew someone was there. I could definitely feel someone's stare."

CONVERSATIONS WITH THE UNKNOWN-OTHER

To understand what the voice of the unknown-other sounds like to the paranoid person, I have combined many examples of how the unknown-other makes itself known, the type of words often used, and the paranoid person's typical response. The following section allows you to "hear" the dialogue, beliefs, and judgments experienced by the paranoid person when they are alone or anxiously stepping out among people. The paranoid person does not initially recognize that there is a connection between one's own intralocution and the voice of the unknown-other.

UNKNOWN-OTHER: What are you doing out here in public? Everyone is staring at you. All these people are watching you and talking about you. What, are you stupid? You can't do anything right.

PARANOID PERSON: Everyone's talking about me? I have to go out; I have to get to work. Shut up and leave me alone. Why is everyone talking about me? I'm trying to do my best.

U-O: Everyone is staring at you. Look at them, looking and laughing at you. You can't hide from us. You are lazy. How can such a lazy man go to work? You'll be fired.

P-P: I'm not lazy. I work. People just never give me a chance.

U-O: We know who you are. You're gay, aren't you? We've suspected that for years. Look how you're dressed. You walk like you're gay. Why are you covering up who you are?

P-P: I can't let anyone know who I am. I know I'm not gay, but I'm afraid people will think I am.

U-O: We are going to attack you, and you're not going to get away. Everyone knows you were molested as a child, and it can be done again. Everyone knows what you do when you're alone. We will spread the news about you. You are such a bastard, a real jerk. No one can stand to look at you.

P-P: I wish everyone would stop talking about my past; I don't want them to know. I've got to keep all this to myself. I'm afraid they will find out about me, and then I'll be made fun of and teased. What if everyone turns against me? I just like to be alone. I need one good friend, that's all.

U-O: No one even likes you, you know that? You used to be someone, but now you're a failure. You can't do anything right. Look at the way you walk, just like a pervert. Everyone knows this about you.

P-P: Just shut up. I'm not a pervert. What they're saying is just not true. If I have to, I'll deny it and just get mad at them. Why is everyone against me?

U-O: Why don't you have a girlfriend? People are wondering about you.

P-P: No one knows; they can assume anything. They don't have to know how lonely I am. They might think I have a girl-friend who owns her own house somewhere else.

U-O: Everyone knows you're a drug addict. They're watching to see what you will steal next. No one trusts you. You don't even take care of your children.

P-P: I'm tired of this all the time. I don't steal anymore. I'm not crazy. I can't let others see me scared all the time. I've got to keep all this to myself.

An interchange occurs that sounds like a disturbing conversation between two people. The paranoid individual believes this voice comes from someone who is watching them; they believe they can actually hear with their ears what that person is thinking and saying about them. The voice of the unknown-other is not a hallucination, no command voice demanding the individual do something, but an emotional voice that expresses how one feels, thinks, regrets, avoids, and pretends in order to remain unaware of oneself.

As you read the following paragraphs, notice I have written it in the personal pronoun, and if a paranoid person is reading this and is recognizing the voice of the unknown-other, their intralocution may jump out at them as they exclaim, "That's me. That's what I go through all the time." This is what a paranoid individual tells me about the conversation they have with the unknown-other.

> "Who are these people who are talking about me? Where do they come from? Why is this voice so negative towards me? Why

are they always putting me down? It's like they can read my mind. Do people really think that bad about me? I am a coward, I know, but how do they know? Is it the way I dress or the way I walk? Does anyone like me the way I am? Why does everyone want me to change?

"This voice appears mostly when I am by myself, out in public, and speaks just loud enough for me to hear it and listen. It's a conversation I have with someone, but they are not standing with me. It seems one-sided and very negative. This voice is a demanding instigator, stirring up trouble and causing problems for me between myself and others. I think it comes from 'over there,' the next street, the person sitting across from me, outside the house I've barricaded with drawn curtains and video surveillance cameras.

"This voice keeps me aware, alert to the dangers that stalk me. No wonder I want to be alone so much. I fear being with people, and I am very distrustful of them. They mean me harm and are trying to do me in. I must protect myself from them. I don't trust anyone. I am all alone. No one else understands. I am always being attacked."

The voice of the unknown-other is the voice of paranoia. It speaks in hush tones or obtrusive screams as this conversation goes on and on within one's intralocution. It's like a battle between enemies, saboteurs, and opponents. The voice of the unknown-other is slowly betraying itself and giving up answers, but it also continues to add negative evaluations.

The paranoid person calls themself names, very derogatory names that epitomize negative self-reflection and self-worth. These names identify what is unacknowledged and unrecognized in oneself, and they will remain unacknowledged until made conscious. The names from the unknown-other are unique to the paranoid individual, and identify what beliefs and attitudes are hidden from conscious awareness and are not yet recognized as self-identities. These words are the unacknowledged, often unacceptable identifiers that one hears from the unknown-other about oneself.

The paranoid person does not want others to learn about these negative thoughts and self-identities. They are both afraid and angry that the unknown-other knows this information and will repeat it and "spread it to others." Their fear and anger help them keep these negative identifiers to themselves. Isolation attempts to silence this voice, often prompting even more fear that others will learn about these unacceptable personality traits. This leads to a stronger and more negative intralocution.

The eyes of the paranoid individual see in two directions. They are always on the lookout for who is watching them, who is out there observing. These same eyes also look inward, into their depths, and inform them of what they shelter and protect. What the eyes see within must be protected from the eyes intent on hurting them. This person does not like you looking into their eyes directly, afraid you will see into them and see their inner inadequacies, weaknesses, and vulnerabilities. They have a lot of negative personal self-identities that they keep to themselves.

They do not want others to know them, fearing they will not approve of them or will find them so unacceptable that they must be rejected. This is all quite embarrassing stuff. The paranoid individual does not want to be identified negatively, yet the negative words they hear in their intralocution are deprecating, disparaging, denigrating, and maligning. The paranoid person lives in fear of others identifying them as their weaknesses, their often scrutinized attitudes and beliefs, and their deprecating self-identities, all of which are also the voice of the unknown-other.

They fear being recognized for what they hate and disapprove about themselves and will do whatever they need to do to keep themselves private. Talking about themself is taking a monumental risk of letting others get close to this "dark side" of their personality, so trusting others is certainly difficult.

JACOB'S STORY

Let us use Jacob's story to explore this seemingly impossible dilemma more fully: keeping one's negative thoughts and beliefs to oneself or expressing one's inner fears out loud.

Now in his twenties, Jacob hears people talk about him everywhere he goes, even when he is not within hearing distance of anyone. He tried therapy for a while to learn to deal with social anxiety. People he hears may be out in the woods hidden from view, someone walking her dog on the other side of the street, or a man in a local pub who is minding his own business. Jacob knows they are all talking about him. Even when he is sitting at home alone, he believes he is the center of people's communication. He doesn't understand why he is in the spotlight and why all the attention is on him.

"Why do they think I'm important enough to talk about?"

He knows others are talking about him because he can hear them. He tells his therapist that one day he was driving down the road in his truck and, looking in his rear-view mirror, could see that a car with two occupants was following him. He could hear the people in the car remark about how lonely he must be since he did not have a girlfriend with him. Jacob gets irate when people talk about him. He could not explain how he knew they were talking about him, but admitted he felt embarrassed that he did not have a girlfriend. Jacob has wanted a girlfriend for many years, and it bothers him greatly that others keep drawing attention to this. He wants desperately to have a girlfriend so others can actually see him with her.

He does not want others to think of him as some weird pervert or sex fiend that cannot keep or satisfy a girl. He remembers having plenty of girls when he was a teen. Even though Jacob is not hearing with his ears, the unknown-other is speaking to him. Jacob wondered, "How do they know I am lonely and desperate for a girlfriend?" He suspected *everyone* was thinking these thoughts about him; he did not even have to see them to know they were talking about him.

Eventually, he hated being seen by anyone because of what the unknown-other was saying to him, so he kept more and more to himself. He did not trust women, but he still felt he deserved a girlfriend. He says his life would be complete with a girlfriend.

One day, he was walking his dog when he spotted a group of teen girls standing on the corner talking. He decided to take a chance and walk by them. They began talking and told him how much they liked his dog, and Jacob believed this was a good introduction. One girl then remarked, "You look like the devil with your beard cut that way."

Jacob is shy around girls, and it devastated him that they would equate him to Satan, and he interpreted this to mean he was "weird and perverted." He was offended, but he believed it must be true since none of them wanted him. He admitted that he has called himself a pervert and weird for many years.

There were many things Jacob did not like to talk about in therapy because they scared him. One can only guess at all the derogatory and self-deprecating names Jacob called himself, but from acknowledging what the voice of the unknown-other is saying to him, his low self-esteem was revealed. After recounting this incident—his exchange with the teenage girls—Jacob did not want to continue talking about his personal feelings, his fear, anger, or his inability to have a girlfriend. He eventually stopped talking to his therapist altogether. Now Jacob no longer has a healthy discharge for the voice of the unknown-other. He did not realize it was his own intralocution he was hearing.

PARANOIA AND THE UNKNOWN-OTHER

A major advancement in understanding paranoia as a psychological phenomenon and a lived-experience comes when one identifies the voice of the unknown-other as their own intralocution. When they acknowledge and identify the unknown-other's voice as their own, then they realize they themselves are the one who is so cruel to themself; they are who is so judgmental. Jung speaks of this disharmony within oneself:

> From all states of unconscious contamination and non-differentiation there is begotten a compulsion to be and act in a way contrary to one's own nature. Accordingly a man can neither be at one with himself nor accept responsibility for himself. He feels himself to be in a degrading, unfree, unethical condition. But the disharmony with himself is precisely the neurotic and intolerable condition from which he seeks to be delivered, and deliverance from this condition will come only when he can be and act as he feels is conformable with his true self. People have a feeling for these things, dim and uncertain at first, but growing ever stronger and clearer with progressive development. ...We must recognize that nothing is more difficult to bear with than oneself (Jung, 1953, p. 225).

Jung is speaking about any condition of one's personal nature that is contrary and antagonistic towards oneself, and paranoia fits exactly into the description. Although the voice of the unknown-other may not quiet down completely after understanding one's involvement in one's paranoia, it still speaks its truth/peace. One now knows logically and realistically that there is no one out there who is doing all that judging; the judge is here inside me, as me, my own judgmental intralocution. I am the voice of the unknown-other. Siegel:

> Darkness and solitude invite the feeling. Many people experience it when they are alone in the house at night or walk down an unfamiliar street. Others may have the vague feeling that their life paths are being jeopardized by jealous persons known or unknown. The creature we all fear, the demon of paranoia, is not "out there," but lurking in the shadows of our very own brains. ...Paranoia is a way of perceiving and feeling the world. The paranoid inhabits a different realm of being, one that tilts the world ever so slightly. The senses detect these differences. They sound mental alarms. The paranoid becomes locked in a new mode of thinking, thereafter viewing the world as if trapped in a cell or, yes, even a demon's lair (Siegel, 1994, pp. 7,19).

There is no demon of paranoia save one's own cruel, judgmental, degrading intralocution. One can get trapped in the "lair" of paranoia by not recognizing the voice of the unknown-other as one's own intralocution. One can go on for years believing it is others who are out to get him—relentlessly cruel and judgmental—and that others know everything about them, but these beliefs only keep paranoia dominant, active, and alive.

The personal pronoun: "It is through the words of the unknown-other that I hear my own beliefs, my unexpressed, unacknowledged, and usually undisclosed self-judgment and self-condemnation, which I live out fearfully or angrily in the world. Once I identify the unknown-other's voice as my intralocution, I can pay attention to my thoughts and how negative and judgmental I am. The voice of the unknown-other is telling me what I may already know about myself, but I don't want to acknowledge it. This voice is harsh and cruel, identifying my worst fears and weaknesses, and it knows my vulnerabilities and embarrassments. It does this because it is me, and I have low self-esteem. The words of the unknown-other are the low self-esteem and negative opinions I have of myself. My low opinion involves the oft-hidden, degrading words and negative views I have formed of myself. I am embarrassed by my self-view, and I do not want others to learn of my self-opinion. I avoid people so as not to 'slip up' and possibly disclose my negative inner view and low self-esteem.

"The unknown-other does not care if I am embarrassed or shy, or whether I want the world to know my business; it is there to pronounce the worst of me, and I cower from that. Since the unknown-other knows me and judges me so harshly, I believe others around me have been able to figure me out just by looking at me. I wonder with doubt if I can hide my personal life well enough; therefore, I must hide my body. I cannot let others see me or know what kind of person I am; what I think and do. I stay to myself more, spend my time alone, away from others who I possibly used to, but no longer, trust. I do not want others to judge me or see the worst of me like the unknown-other can. As hard as I may try, I cannot hide from the unknown-other. It always knows where I am. It knows all about me, and that is scary."

As those who are not paranoid read the above descriptions of what it's like to be paranoid, you may now realize that the voice of the unknown-other parallels the often-heard but usually unacknowledged self-talk by the paranoid individual's intralocution. It is not someone else, someone "out there." Paranoia is a self-evaluation—usually negative, judgmental, and harsh—and it identifies and points to areas of the personality and belief system that are weak and inferior. Paranoia is self-scrutiny, of which one may not be self-aware. David Shapiro (1981) states it this way:

> ...the projective identification of the enemy in the shadows can be seen as the product of a nervous, defensively searching and interpreting—suspicious—attention (p. 37). ...When the content of projective ideas is actually essentially the same as the content of the original internal concern... the form of the original internal experience, a self-critical judgment, happens to be identical with the form of the later defensive concern. The original internal tension, in other words, is already a critical self-consciousness; ...and the defensive concern or projective idea generated involves only the substitution of an external figure for the individual's own self-consciousness (p. 144).

In psychoanalytic terms, it is a projection onto others of one's own thinking and beliefs, but this is unacknowledged and unrecognized[16] until one makes it conscious. But projection does not fully explain paranoia and is only a construct that pre-

---

[16] Projection is one of several defense mechanisms, and Freud defines these as unconscious methods one uses to protect oneself from consciously having to deal with one's anxiety, one's difficult issues and situations.

vents us from fully appreciating paranoia for what it truly is. The construct of projection gives us an understanding of what one does to prevent oneself from recognizing and accepting the persecutor as oneself, but it blinds us from understanding who the victim of paranoia is, and why we believe "they" are the ones who are truly saying these terrible things about us.

Initially, one does not believe that they, themselves, are creating their own paranoia. As one becomes more comfortable talking about and accepting one's paranoia, one will rid oneself of the term "unknown-other." But I believe, initially, it is a useful term to help enlighten and gather personal insight about one's negative, degrading self-esteem. It helps explain how the paranoid mind thinks and who one believes is initially at the root of one's suspiciousness.

SUMMARY

The voice of the unknown-other is actually my own thoughts, but at first, I do not realize this; I believe it is another person. I believe I can hear what others are thinking and saying about me. If I listen to the words of the unknown-other, and acknowledge what the unknown-other is saying, I can become conscious of what I say and believe about myself.

> ...it begins to put on these others—people who are outside of him, his enemies—everything which he has clearly formulated in himself as defect, blamable weakness, and so on. Thus, as the process goes on, he begins to wash his hands of all those real and fancied unfortunate aspects of his own personality which he has suffered for up to this time. Under those circumstances, needless to say, he arrives at a state which

is pretty hard to remedy—by categorical
name, a paranoid state (Sullivan, 1953,
p. 362).

"I am the voice of paranoia, manifesting in my life as I
continually withdraw from others through anger, fear, distrust,
suspiciousness, loneliness, and low self-esteem, but this changes
after I recognize this truth. Once recognized as myself, paranoia can then become the inspiration to inform and instruct me
about many facets of my life and personality that need attention
and correction." We will pursue this transformative use of paranoia in a later chapter.

SELF-ESTEEM

The paranoid individual has low self-esteem and poor self-image, believing they must protect themself from being seen and judged by others. They believe others judge them harshly and that they look down on them. They do not put themself "out there" for fear they will be questioned about themself, and they will realize they are as worthless as they believe they are. They fear they will be proven to be a fraud. The paranoid person thinks everyone is a critic, a spy, a nosy reporter looking for dirt to spread around. They believe themself to be *subhuman*, a step below humanity, and thus it is difficult for them to be around others.

They speak negatively to themself, call themself injurious names, and usually have no one around to question the validity of their antagonistic, self-defeating inner voice. Their paranoia did not develop overnight or even over a few months. Paranoia grows, supported by negative self-esteem and low self-image. When one believes one is incapable, inefficient, or inherently "less than" others, one has planted a seed of paranoia. Loneliness and distrust help germinate paranoia fully.

Paranoid people look out into the world and believe others are more accomplished, better looking, more talented, and threatening. They live by the credo that there is something inherently wrong with them; "Does everyone know how messed up I am?" They believe negatively about themselves, their abilities and capabilities, and do not want anyone to discover this. They fear that if others know too much about them, both positive and negative, it will be used against them. They imagine the most shameful things about themselves, and they must protect these sensitivities, and this foretells our study of low self-esteem and how it influences paranoia.

UNDERSTANDING SELF-ESTEEM

The study of self-esteem is problematic since there is no clear understanding of what it is. Literally, hundreds of books and articles are devoted to explaining and understanding self-esteem and all it entails. So many self-help books are available but trying to get a concise understanding of what we understand as self-esteem is greatly lacking. Some researchers feel self-esteem is of utmost importance to understand one's involvement in life and one's interactions with society, while at the same time, some believe self-esteem has little value in affecting behavior or long-term consequences.

> In the past 30 years, self-esteem has become deeply embedded in popular culture, championed as the royal road to happiness and personal fulfillment, and touted as an antidote to a variety of social ills, including unemployment, gang violence, and teenage pregnancy. Despite its widespread usage within nonacademic circles, academic psychologists have been divided with respect to self-esteem's function and benefits. While some argue that high self-esteem is essential to human functioning and imbues

life with meaning, others assert that it is of
little value and may actually be a liability
(Brown & Marshall, 2006).

In their short and very thoughtful paper, Brown and
Marshall first define *global* self-esteem as how people generally
feel about themselves, as it endures across time and situations.
The paranoid person feels negative about themself, believing
they are not okay or well-liked, not just today, but this has been
their personal view, possibly for years. The second way Brown
and Marshall define self-esteem is the feeling of self-worth,
focusing on the emotions expressed at the time, and how they
"feel" positive or negative about themselves. The paranoid individual may feel either positive or negative about themself, but
this can change in a flash. Their self-esteem is very sensitive and
can turn from "I'm okay" to feeling devastated quickly with just
another's glance or remark, or a negative thought of their own.

And third, Brown & Marshall define self-esteem as one's
self-evaluation. One tests one's abilities to do something well or
not so well, and this is one's self-evaluation, one's self-esteem.
I describe later in this chapter how self-efficacy is a method of
self-evaluation that the paranoid individual uses to "prove" to
themself that they are inferior to others.

Self-esteem is typically thought of as an indication of
how one thinks, feels, and judges oneself. Positive self-esteem
has been shown to positively correlate with one's psychological
health. Positive self-esteemed individuals are genuinely happier
than others and less depressed. They are more persistent in the
face of challenges (Baumeister, Campbell, Krueger, & Vohs,
2005). Negative self-esteemed individuals tend to be depressed,
fearful and angry, disillusioned about the world, and undoubt-
edly egocentric. But what is self-esteem, really? Is it only with
our positive or negative feelings that we judge ourselves? Must
we judge ourselves among other people to determine how we
feel about ourselves, or can we truly know our self-esteem in

isolation, without others' influence? Can one's perception of and reaction to fear, anxiety, and life experience affect self-esteem, and can self-esteem change over time?

A study of self-esteem can be quite complicated. As a constituent of paranoia, though, self-esteem has much to say. It helps us understand how paranoid individuals think and feel about themselves and how they believe others think about and judge them as well.

I am not about to redefine self-esteem, its meaning, or its involvement in other aspects of life, but I will focus on it as a constituent of paranoia. To what degree one's self-esteem is positive or negative does not have to be refined or understood in any more rigid detail. As I use the term *self-esteem* in this chapter, I am typically talking about a conglomeration of the three ways defined by Brown and Marshall. I separate self-esteem into two categories: **pseudo** (false, fake, egocentric, easily influenced by others—both positive and negative) and **authentic** (true, honest, self-respected, actualized through integrity). I discuss how both negative and positive self-esteem affects the paranoid individual but spotlight how the paranoid individual has negative self-esteem in greater supply. Authentic self-esteem may be the long-term goal and impetus for abandoning paranoia as a coping mechanism.

SELF-ESTEEM AND ANXIETY

As has been consistent throughout this book, I believe one must address anxiety and its power and influence over one's life. Anxiety is a force to be reckoned with before and alongside all the ups and downs of our self-esteem. Anxiety does not create positive or negative self-esteem, but self-esteem can be influenced by our successes or failed attempts at handling anxiety. Anxiety may make us run from situations and people who challenge us. Over time, if we confront our anxiety by learning to understand it, confronting our fears, and dealing with life without retreating from it, we may develop a deeper understanding and apperception of anxiety's influence.

One phenomenon that has been increasing over the past few decades is children having an especially tough time dealing with anxiety and choosing instead to retreat to playing video games, often alone in the dark. Before the onslaught of video games, children had to confront their anxiety and face their fears, or the anxiety would overwhelm them. If they pushed themselves through different and difficult anxious moments, they learned who they were and what they were capable of accomplishing. Children learn their true inner strengths by confronting tense situations.

It also benefits them if they have a mature adult in their life who can help them deal with and better understand how to handle anxiety and how it affects their lives. Video game playing does not influence authentic self-esteem, but it does pseudo self-esteem. Many chronic video-playing kids cannot have meaningful relationships in the actual "real" world but instead develop "internet" friendships with other individuals who may equally be in the dark, whom they have never met, but call "friends." They may be able to speak with others in virtual reality but not in real human-to-human interaction. Anxious children would profit by dealing with their anxiety, pushing themselves through the difficult face-to-face encounters, and learning from those experiences, slowly coming to realize that they can survive anxiety and accomplish much success.

SELF-ESTEEM AND BELIEFS

In a previous chapter, I showed how "meaning" is the interrelationship between people, things, places, times, etc. Self-esteem *is* one of these relationships; it is a relationship one has with oneself. It is a meaning of ourselves to ourselves. We can believe anything we want about ourselves, ranging the gamete from positive to negative, but believing something does not make it true or accurate. If one wants to believe they are the greatest human God has put on earth, the inflated ego will speak and try to convince oneself that this is true (positive pseudo self-esteem). If one believes, "I ain't worth shit," that is the deflated ego speaking (negative pseudo self-esteem).

Can one know one's true self-esteem without inflation or deflation? Low self-esteem is negative self-evaluation. The low self-esteemed individual believes themself to be less than and incompatible around others. Others always seem to be better looking, more talented, have an easier time in life, are more motivated, have better chances of getting the job, have better luck, and are happier. The low self-esteemed individual may be more depressed and show a lot of fear or anger.[17]

They are afraid of making mistakes and being seen as "not good enough." They are not good enough to win or to be recognized for anything special. They believe others look down on them and think negatively about them. They are sensitive to what others say. They believe they "know" what others are thinking about them. They feel inadequate, "less than" others, and they put themself down in the same way they believe others put them down. They do unto themself as they believe others do unto them.

They lack the self-confidence to try something they have never done before, and they feel useless if they are not good at anything they try. When challenged, they eventually give up and say, "Why bother?" or "I don't care." They do not care anymore about excelling at difficult projects, for that may expose their weaknesses. They are tired of being made fun of—whether by actual people or their own intralocution—and they continue

---

[17] Remember from a previous chapter that anger and fear are both present, but one is on the surface while the other is mostly restricted and held prisoner inside, possibly even unconscious.

to judge themself negatively. The low self-esteemed individual has given up on trying due to too many defeats.

Comparing who we are among others, even if we are less accomplished or have not fully achieved what we intend to do, does not necessarily mean self-esteem is lacking. Through days, months, and years, the immature person adjusts their self-beliefs based on how they perceive themselves among others, but this is pseudo self-esteem. If I believe others are better than me, are they actually better? Better than what? Better than who? It is quite possible to be more skillful at some activity, some talent, and some intellectual pursuit, but no one can claim to be perfect and good at everything, not without touching the delusional.

Personal pronoun speaking: "If I never speak about my beliefs to others, then I may be delusional. I can believe that I am a great and beautiful singer and that I am well-loved by everyone, but when I test my beliefs among others, these may prove delusional, false, and inflated self-beliefs that have no energy, life, proof, or truth except in my narrow belief system. I may not be as important as I believe I am, only in my mind." A belief proves nothing but says much about the person doing the believing. "I need to experience myself among healthy individuals, not other paranoid people."

EXAMPLES OF LOW SELF-ESTEEM

Here is an example of a young woman with low self-esteem. Lana is a writer who has written her first novel, but she hesitates for two years to seek a publisher, even though her close friends tell her the book is good, interesting, and well-written. She believes she has no talent and is incapable of being published. She does not share her friends' opinions, believing negatively about herself that others do not share. She puts herself down and belittles her talent. Lana does not want to risk her already low self-esteem and find out it may be true. Unless Lana confronts her fear and exposes her worries and concerns, she will not know for certain if her low self-esteem is accurate; if feeling defeated and worthless is the true meaning of her life to herself.

In reality, she has written a novel, but her thoughts tell her not to expose herself to others' opinions, which she fears may be negative as well. Talent and ability can be real, but self-esteem may not be authentic until it is demonstrated, among others, over time. Must one get out among other people to bring to light what one knows as one's self-esteem? Do we experience our self-esteem when we are among others?

Jane, a grown woman, tells me that she wanted to help her mother in the kitchen with baking when she was young, but her mother had no tolerance for messiness. One day, Jane's mother was preparing a cake for father's birthday, and Jane asked if she could help. Her mother said, "No, but you can watch." Jane felt bad just sitting there watching, not contributing to the creation of the birthday cake.

At the celebration later that evening, mother brought in the cake and announced, "Janie helped me prepare this beautiful cake." Jane was not fooled. She knew she had nothing to do with preparing that cake. Even though she was thanked and told what a wonderful job she did, she felt sad and mad. She felt small, belittled, lied to, and deceived. She says whatever self-esteem she had plummeted. This was evidence to her that she was no better than her low self-esteem informed. Her self-confidence was low. The mature Jane now realizes that she did not accept the fake praise, but she accepted the low self-esteem. She felt as if she was living a lie.

One more example of low self-esteem: Shane has been in therapy for depression and is coming to acknowledge his low self-esteem. Shane's confidence and self-esteem should be high from all obvious external indications since he has a small collection of good friends, is gifted in sports, enjoys creating music, and excels academically. Yet, he acknowledges that his self-judgment is negative.

He repeatedly tells himself, "You're a nobody. You can't do anything right." Even when he hits a home run, he tells himself, "That's not so great; anyone can do it." He does not believe he is a successful baseball player, even with a .295 lifetime average, so far. He does not like to hear praise from others and gets upset if anyone wants to offer help with anything he's doing. He prefers to do everything alone and to be left alone. He has been distancing himself from his friends. He does not believe others when they tell him they enjoy listening to him play his guitar.

How can we understand Shane's low self-esteem when the outside appearance of his life seems positive, well-accomplished, and strong? In this case, it would probably be better not to limit our focus to low self-esteem only. Shane has low self-esteem, but there is something more insidious besides his low self-esteem issues, something that has low self-esteem incorporated into its structure.

Since this chapter is on self-esteem and its connection with paranoia, I use this example to show the influence of low self-esteem on one's life and the difficulty of recognizing paranoia when it is not overtly obvious. When we examine the bigger picture of Shane's life, he gives us a look at a developing paranoid personality. Focusing for a moment on his low self-esteem and understanding it as a constituent of the structure of paranoia helps us understand Shane's negative view of himself, considering the other paranoia constituents.

EVALUATING SELF-ESTEEM

Do you feel good about who *you* are? Do you approve of yourself? Do you believe all humans are meant to have good self-esteem?

> The need to see ourselves as good is the
> need to experience self-respect. It emerges

very early. As we develop from childhood, we progressively become aware of the power to choose our actions. We become aware of our responsibility for the choices we make. We acquire our sense of being a person. We experience a need to feel that we are right—*right as a person*—right in our characteristic way of functioning. This is the need to feel that we are *good* (Branden, 1994, p. 39).

Do you see disappointment, failure, immoral values, and a lack of integrity in yourself? Although this type of negative, degrading, low opinion one has of oneself may be true, it is low self-esteem, what is referred to here as pseudo self-esteem. Pseudo self-esteem can be true, as evidenced by the life one lives, often substantiated in one's mind, and it is regressive. It is what one believes about oneself that is negative. But as we know, not everyone's opinion of oneself is negative. One may be quite positive, happy with oneself, everything setting well, accomplished, and looking up. In the extreme, one may feel overly positive, in fact, to the point that one believes one is special, exceptional, superior, the ultra-human that everyone adores.

Pseudo self-esteem is divided into two categories—low and high. People with low self-esteem experience negative pseudo self-esteem, while those who experience inflated and grandiose self-esteem experience positive pseudo self-esteem, possibly developing narcissism.

Suspicion abounds where low self-esteem lives. The paranoid person sounds like this: "Who can I trust? What are *they* up to? I am at the bottom of the heap, and I believe everyone knows this. I believe others are so interested in belittling and humiliating me, it's best that I just avoid them. This is why I am alone. I am so inadequate and worthless that others are always trying to take advantage of me. They will pounce, attach, and make it known how useless I am at the first opportunity. How do they know how inadequate I am? They just know. I put myself down just like they do to me. Why should I trust them? I hear what they say about me. I'm afraid of being found out and exposed. No wonder people spy on me and are out to get me. They are out to annihilate me, embarrass me, do away with me. I am no good. No one wants me. I hate myself so much, even *I* don't want to be my own friend. It is best that I stay alone, out of sight. I live this way all the time."

What underlies negative, depressive, low self-esteem, and how does this happen? The literature suggests that abuse, put-downs, belittling, anger toward oneself, frustration, lack of emotional support, no one to talk to, bullying, feeling disparate from others at a young age, believing that one doesn't matter, plus other personal and influential negative beliefs, all contribute to low self-esteem. With this lengthy but partial list of negative influences affecting one's self-esteem, is it any wonder that we all have low self-esteem at times?

> That is, people with low self-esteem are not merely down on themselves; they are negative about everything (Baumeister, Campbell, Krueger, & Vohs, 2005).

One's pseudo self-esteem can be negatively influenced just by being around other low self-esteemed people. It is difficult to be around negative, condescending, and condemning people, who have little to say that is positive about anything, and who are dealing with their own low self-esteem issues. Some people work hard to prevent low self-esteem from taking over their life, but many cannot raise themselves up legitimately to believe they are worthwhile and important. They may continue, possibly permanently, to be negative toward themselves in their self-belief and self-judgment.

Self-Esteem in Childhood

What if we judge ourselves only by the reputation of our previous self, our self from the past? Did the child develop self-esteem through ridicule, taunting, belittling, or did they receive positive emotional support? How can we help a child develop positive self-esteem and build confidence and ability without falling into the trap of praising his ego and hence puffing him up falsely? What effect does nurture have on self-esteem?

How one is raised influences one's self-esteem, both pseudo and authentic. Were you raised to feel positive and hopeful, or did negative self-esteem influences rule your life? Were you treated unfairly as a child, pushed toward failure, or set up with tough and unrealistic goals? Were you made to feel unwanted and unloved, bullied and belittled? Exposed to authoritarian parenting, too many rules, and no power or permission to voice your thoughts and feelings? Various events in life can negatively influence and change one's opinion of oneself for the worse.

> Presumably, the emerging roots of a healthy and constructive self-esteem are nourished by those developmental experiences in which the child feels himself to be valued, loved, and cherished by the powerful and significant objects who form the matrix of his developmental experience. ...Basic trust can be seen as a fundamental form of self-regard that contributes substantially to the emerging sense of self-esteem. ...If this emerging self-expression is met with excessively punitive rejection or harsh restriction, the emerging sense of self is correspondingly injured. The result is often an abiding sense of self-doubt, shame, and inferiority or inadequacy (Meissner, 1986, p. 96).

A self-esteem movement in the 1980s promoted self-praise through self-talk and aggrandizement from parents and teachers. It has escaped the 1980s and can still be witnessed today in parenting and schools. Did the "I'm wonderful and special" and "I love myself" affirmations that took hold a few decades ago uplift or sentence children to a lifelong struggle to overcome ego-based, pseudo self-esteem instead of the more formidable and worthwhile authentic self-esteem?

A child needs acceptance, unconditional love, pride in what they do, and a certain number of rules and discipline to keep their behavior good and from swelling their ego. The belief was that through inflation of children's egos, praising them for everything they did, whether they were successful or not, was a step toward genuine, authentic self-esteem and success, but it was not. What was accomplished was an inflated ego, narcissistic thinking and behaviors, self-absorption, and feelings of entitlement. Even though the intention was meant to create positive self-esteem, it backfired. This resulting inflated ego (positive, pseudo) has nothing to do with authentic self-esteem. This "I am perfect" self-esteem is pseudo self-esteem, not based on reality, fact, or accomplished living.

> Self-esteem can never be simply implanted by others' comments, but it can be interfered with by too much criticism or too much unearned praise. Today's parents tend to offer too much approval and enthusiasm for their children's very existence, disrupting the child's growing ability to discern the truth about her own effects and actions. Effusively praising every step she takes, every task she completes, every soccer play she executes, and every book she reads fosters the self-esteem trap. If nothing is expected as an ordinary

part of becoming a civilized member of a
human group, then a child may come to
feel important for breathing—a belief that
will not serve her well (Young-Eisendrath,
2008, p. 31).

A spoiled child's ego swells so much that their egocentric,
pseudo self-esteem becomes very difficult to deal with. They
expect privileges that have not been earned; they want their
freedom before they are capable of handling it, and they think
greater of themselves than they do others.

Too much parental praise for grades,
appearance, thinness, wit, and athletic
or musical performance interferes with
a child's feeling ordinary and in fact can
interrupt the development of self-deter-
mination by creating an intense hunger
for admiration or approval from others,
as we have seen. Feeding our children
"junk praise" is similar to feeding them
junk food that spawns unhealthy cravings.
Under these conditions, a person cannot
easily learn from experience... (Young-
Eisendrath, 2008, p. 125).

A seven-year-old child should be treated as a typical seven-year-old child, not too special and not made to feel above
their peers. A sixteen-year-old teenager should be treated as a
typical sixteen-year-old, not as an adult with adult freedoms
and privileges, and they certainly should not be reduced to
being treated like a younger child, immature without responsibilities or greater expectations. Believe it or not, most young-
sters are ordinary, typical children, nothing more special about
them than other children of the same age. We are cognizant of

unique talents, abilities, and capabilities in sports, music, art, or academics. These make a child unique and individual. But with human-to-human comparison, each child is just as special and ordinary as the rest of the children their age.

SELF-ESTEEM AND NARCISSISM

This book is about paranoia, not narcissism, but as a general overarching principle, the main difference between paranoia and narcissism is through the manifestation of pseudo self-esteem, be it negative or positive. With inflated pseudo self-esteem, one thinks oneself better than others, i.e., "special," that one is different and separate from others: narcissistic. The narcissist believes they are superior, better, above others because they believe in their positive pseudo self-esteem.[18]

A life built on pseudo self-esteem, be it positive or negative, is like a house built on sand; it may have no genuine support in reality and may not stand up to the experience of real authentic self-esteem. If I am told I am special or I tell myself I am better than others, but without solid and sustainable accomplishment, then my ego is inflated, and I move along the scale toward positive pseudo self-esteem. If I am often told, or I tell myself, I am inferior, not good, a "low life," then I move myself along the scale toward negative pseudo self-esteem. When a child takes part in creative activities, the chance of improving their positive self-esteem increases. Authentic self-esteem is part of something doable, observable, and physically experienced, and it must be an activity one can actually accomplish, not just a thought, hope, or imagination. As Rogers says:

---

[18] The narcissist may feel lonely because of their belief that they are better than others and no one can get emotionally close to them because they believe they are so good, powerful, and superior to others. There is loneliness with this kind of belief. "I have no equal. Who can I trust?" Loneliness and distrust exist for both narcissism and paranoia.

> Creativity always has the stamp of the indi-
> vidual upon its product, but the product is
> not the individual, not his materials, but
> partakes of the relationship between the
> two (Rogers, 1961, p. 349).

Self-esteem, like creativity, must be lived out in life, not just within one's thinking or imagination.

Authentic Self-Esteem

As the child gets their life together, they contribute to the pseudo or authentic understanding of themself and their self-esteem. Authentic self-esteem is not something anyone can just give you; it develops according to your mature thoughts, attitudes, beliefs, and hopes. One looks back over their life and sees the progression they made, and they are satisfied. If they are not satisfied, they still have work to do on themself. Therapeutically, they may need to delve into aspects of their life that they could not mature or develop fully, aspects that still hold them to their childhood. Authentic self-esteem develops and matures as we grow. Once established, authentic self-esteem is strong; it is not permanently weakened by off-handed comments, difficulties of life, or by loss or gain. It is less influenced by the movements of the ego. During a temporary life setback, authentic self-esteem is still strong, formidable, and lasting; it is a long-term achievement.

We cannot sufficiently or accurately change our self-esteem by buying new clothes, a flashy sports car, a new house, a different hairstyle, having a beautiful partner, or possessing more money than our neighbors. This attitude only supports ego-based, pseudo self-esteem, and it is volatile and fleeting. It can change quickly. The raising of one's authentic self-esteem is the creative process. It requires one to work for what one is capable of doing and creating. We may use our imagination and creativity to picture ourselves being sufficient, good, productive, etc., but it cannot stay in our imagination to be effective. It must be manifested, acted, lived, and tested out there in the world. If it remains only in imagination, it is pseudo self-esteem.

If our view and self-judgment stand the test of time, we call it authentic self-esteem if it can be shown to be correct and obvious to ourselves and others. When we are isolated and believe our self-esteem is positive, this is pseudo. Whenever we build ourselves up without substantial outside proof that we deserve it, we falsely inflate our ego. The difference between pseudo self-esteem and authentic self-esteem is in how we live. When one makes the conscious effort to accept oneself, with all of one's ordinariness and struggles, one lays the foundation of self-acceptance, flaws and all. One can then live life with integrity, authenticity, and kindness to self and others.

Real, authentic self-esteem is genuine, and it cannot be faked. Genuine, authentic self-esteem is in the way we live: fully, wholly, honestly, and integrated. It is not something different from who we are. Authentic self-esteem takes much work to achieve. One begins by taking all aspects of one's life seriously and reworking those aspects that do not conform to whom one is as a unique individual. Branden identifies "pillars" of self-esteem and how one can live as an honest, authentic person: with both self-acceptance and acceptance of others.

> Self-efficacy and self-respect are the dual pillars of healthy self-esteem (Branden, 1994, p. 27).

One begins to identify with the personal practice of living consciously, with conscious self-acceptance, self-responsibility, self-assertiveness, living purposefully, and with personal integrity as the roots, the *pillars*, of authentic self-esteem.

Once we understand these practices, we
have the power to choose them and work
on integrating them into our way of life.
The power to do so is the power to raise
the level of our self-esteem, from whatever
point we may be starting and however difficult the project may be in the early stages.
One does not have to attain "perfection"
in these practices. One only needs to raise
one's average level of performance to experience growth in self-efficacy and self-re-
spect (Branden, 1994, p. 65).

Authentic self-esteem is demonstrated in the way one
lives; it cannot only be imagined or believed to be genuine. We
expose our authentic self-esteem in our way of living among
others through our identity and personhood. We can believe
whatever we want about ourselves, but authentic self-esteem
is not fooled. If we cannot live our authentic self-esteem and
abilities, then there are self-doubts and questions about what
is true, real, and authentic, and we have moved closer to living
pseudo self-esteem. Authentic self-esteem needs to rise out of
our authentic and genuine way of living.

We are not in this world alone; we live among others, and
our interaction with others partially helps determine our self-esteem. There is a close connection between our self-esteem and
our self-efficacy. We understand:

Self-efficacy means confidence in the functioning of my mind, in my ability to think,
understand, learn, choose, and make decisions, confidence in my ability to understand the facts of reality that fall within the
sphere of my interests and needs; self-trust;
self-reliance (Branden, 1994, p. 26).

If a person is good at something, even trivial things, and given the time necessary to develop and grow one's ability, accomplishment, accuracy, and skill, then their self-efficacy also relates to their self-esteem. With authentic self-esteem, one can talk with others about their ability and interests, feel confident in their knowledge, and are willing to demonstrate their ability among others. Conversely, if they do not feel accomplished in something and lack the skills necessary to feel adequate around others, their self-esteem is diminished. We are again referring to pseudo self-esteem. Authentic self-esteem develops over the years and is an integration of who we are *in potentia*.

> Pseudo self-esteem is the illusion of self-efficacy and self-respect without the reality. It is a nonrational, self-protective device to diminish anxiety and to provide a spurious sense of security—to assuage our need for authentic self-esteem while allowing the real causes of its lack to remain unexamined (Branden, 1994, p. 51).

If one avoids even the minimal ability in their life, then they will suffer lower self-esteem. If one is generally good at things, be it sports, academics, artistry, speaking skills, etc., they will feel positive about themself among others and have positive self-esteem. One can be good at something, but if they do not share their talents or ideas, what purpose are those talents? The low self-esteemed individual keeps whatever they have developed to themself. They hide themself from the world. They may be talented, but if they keep it "hidden under a basket," that light will not contribute to others or to the world around them. Talent, understanding, ability, creativity, and knowledge all must be shared.

Truth becomes reality only as the individual produces it in action, which includes producing it in his own consciousness (May, 1983, pp. 72-73).

When one turns toward learning about oneself and improving one's psychological health, then one is working toward authentic self-esteem. When we develop the skills to verbally and artistically articulate what we know, think, and do, we approach more highly refined self-esteem. One must put themself out there to be seen by others, to be "judged" among others. Do they feel like they fit in? Self-evaluation promotes self-esteem, either pseudo or authentic. How we feel about ourselves while in the world is our self-evaluation. If we only stay in our head, behind closed doors, and shut off from community, we may judge ourselves as less than or possibly better than others, when compared to an actual personal, human-to-human interaction. Self-esteem is both self-evaluation and self-judgment, but without other people, what is our touchstone from which our personal gold standard can be determined?

Taking care of ourselves is the task we set before ourselves if we intend to develop authentic self-esteem. Care is the undertaking of treating others as we treat ourselves, and treating ourselves as we treat others; with respect, kindness, integrity, compassion, and emotional toughness when needed.

You discover your strengths and weaknesses from the effects of your actions in the world (what you do and produce) and how others see you, reporting back to you what your influence has been on them. Good self-esteem comes from actual accomplishments and relationships; it is the by-product of doing some things well, accepting your limitations (when you need help from others), and seeing the good consequences of your own influences (Young-Eisendrath, 2008, p. 31).

Gimmicks, worksheet exercises, magazine checklists, and external praise do not work to increase authentic self-esteem. Verbal exercises and repeated positive affirmations work to increase *pseudo* self-esteem. These inflate the ego because they may not be based on how one actually lives or knows oneself. Affirmations try convincing oneself of something based on one's wishful imagination, not on living facts. With true, authentic self-esteem, one not only feels one has a positive self-image; one lives one's positive self-esteem and self-image in all other aspects of one's life. As one matures, the ever-important structure of a healthy personality begins to emerge and contributes to rising self-esteem, as described by Brandon.

> Since self-esteem is *a consequence*, a product of internally generated practices, we cannot work on self-esteem *directly*, neither our own nor anyone else's. We must address ourselves to the source. If we understand what these practices are, we can commit to *initiating* them within ourselves and to dealing with others in such a way as to *facilitate* or *encourage* them to do likewise (Branden, 1994, p. 65).

Self-Esteem and Paranoia

The paranoid individual has low self-esteem. They spend their time thinking about how inadequate they are around others. If they are wise, they stop blaming others for making them feel low and inadequate. But if they do not consciously realize they are doing this, they will blame others for talking about them. Paranoia is a vicious cycle of self-blame and self-condemnation. Paranoid people talk to themselves in very negative terms. "I am insignificant and unimportant." (Repeat something like this to yourself 100 times today, tomorrow, and for the next year, and see if it changes your self-esteem.) They believe they can do no good, they are no good, and they cannot compete with others.

They experience low self-esteem and believe others are better. They are inadequate to be around and associate with others. They acknowledge that others look down on them, and their low self-esteem agrees with that. This is the trap, their cycle of self-ridicule, self-indignity, and disesteem. They are not comfortable out there in the world, among others. They remain isolated, filled with self-doubt, and distrustful. They live with pseudo self-esteem, possibly completely out of touch and unaware of any genuine, authentic self-esteem that potentially exists within their abilities and personality. They feel inadequate and believe others are better, smarter, gifted, and cunning, and if they aren't careful, others will show their superiority and embarrass them at any opportunity. They believe others talk about them, ridicule them, and just know that they are inadequate and inferior. Without companionship, they have no means of validating or invalidating what they believe about themself.

The paranoid individual lives a vicious cycle. They do not and cannot trust others out of fear that others will discover their inadequacies, low self-esteem, faults, and negative self-beliefs. They fear what others can do to them. Thus, since they cannot trust others, they believe they must stay apart from them, out of the spotlight, alone, isolated. They believe it is safer. Their thoughts are negative, and their self-esteem lowers even more.

Authentic self-esteem is not a *comparison* of one person against another. True authentic self-esteem emerges from the way one lives in a caring relationship with the world. Just because one is good at something, has talents, or is considered "gifted," does not mean they are *better*, a superior person in any regard. As we mature, we may decide to stay away from the game of "ego comparison," that we are just not interested in comparing ourselves with others anymore. We know that any real comparison among people only separates, not unites. Staying away from comparing ourselves with others provides the opportunity for genuine, authentic self-esteem to emerge.

In therapy, we focus on our deep emotional concerns and inadequacies, areas of life where we are lacking, on our significant relationships, and our long-term personal desires to overcome whatever pseudo self-esteem has been shadowing us. We encounter all the negative thoughts, beliefs, memories, and emotions that previously dominated our lives. We work toward developing our authentic self-esteem, making our life, as we live it, our self-esteem. We are becoming *authentic human beings,* and our personality will begin reflecting that. True, authentic self-esteem needs to grow and build over a lifetime. It matures as we mature. Young-Eisendrath:

> Like honesty, authenticity is a virtue that is initially hard to understand from the outside. If you're focused on external success, manipulating others, or status, it's very hard to see the value of being authentic: the quality of being transparent and open, honest and genuine. ...when something is authentic, it is genuine, worthy of trust, and grounded in truth or fact (Young-Eisendrath, 2008, p. 103).

SUMMARY

Pseudo self-esteem is flimsy, easily altered, up and down, ego-comparative, and can change with any positive or negative comment. Negative pseudo self-esteem is immature, often kept to oneself and seldom shared. One thinks of oneself as inadequate around others. Positive pseudo self-esteem is still immature because one believes oneself to be better than others, special and superior in some sense.

True authentic self-esteem is not stagnant or stationary. It incorporates our genuine self and how we live it among other people. Authentic self-esteem is mature, positive, kind, supportive, moral, and self-actualized. It takes other people into account. It accepts our past negative immature self and says, "I've changed, I'm better at being an ordinary human being now, and I live a better version of myself." And this becomes real, lived out authentically, having required a great deal of inner personal struggle to achieve.

Authentic self-esteem is based on a verifiable, powerful sense of who one is; it is slow to build, life-affirming, and integrates all aspects of one's life, including our social life. We make evident who we are, our true self-esteem, when we are part of the community.

THE COMPLEX

UNTIL THIS POINT IN THE book, I have not needed to delve into the construct of the *unconscious* mind too deeply. I used it briefly to explain anxiety and how it works from beneath the "I don't know" of conscious life. It can be a useful tool for understanding the psyche in the sense that Jung and Freud had used the term. Some theorists do not believe there is an unconscious mind, or that there is any need to consider that our mind may contain an unconscious counterpart.

Van den Berg defines the meaning of unconscious as "self-concealment"; hence, he found no need to use the term to understand human psychology. I have found that using the accepted psychoanalytic meanings of the unconscious mind is very helpful and useful to more fully grasp a deeper understanding of paranoia. I am using my research and understanding of paranoia to explore the thoughts, feelings, and behaviors of paranoia and also the hidden and consciously unknown aspects of the paranoid individual's life.

In this chapter, I will explore how one's mind is not only conscious but also unconscious of many aspects of life, which will benefit a deeper understanding of paranoia. The unconscious is a portion of the mind that is not conscious but remains powerfully influential in one's daily life. Jung writes:

So defined, the unconscious depicts an
extremely fluid state of affairs: everything
of which I know, but of which I am not at
the moment thinking; everything of which
I was once conscious but have now forgotten; everything perceived by my senses, but
not noted by my conscious mind; everything which, involuntarily and without
paying attention to it, I feel, think, remember, want, and do; all the future things that
are taking shape in me and will sometime
come to consciousness: all this is the content of the unconscious. These contents
are all more or less capable, so to speak,
of consciousness, or were once conscious
and may become conscious again the next
moment (Jung, 1960/1969, p. 185).

As we understand this concept, the unconscious mind
comprises ideas, moments, and events that have been forgotten,
suppressed, or repressed. If I do not or cannot think about an
experience because it holds too much emotion, suppression is
the way to eject it from my conscious mind. I then will not let
it bother me or knowingly influence me. Freud used the word
repression to describe a defense mechanism that *automatically*
rejects ideas, thoughts, or memories from our conscious mind,
ones that may evoke too much anxiety or emotional reaction.
For example, the anxiety related to the fear of death and dying
is often quickly repressed by the faint of heart because of the
tremendous anxiety it can evoke.

A therapist tends to understand the client according to
their theoretical leaning, be it behavioral, humanistic, existential, Jungian, psychodynamic, medical, cognitive, etc. The concept of the *complex* and the unconscious are explained throughout Jung's writings, and his argument for the use of the complex

as a psychological tool is convincing. In a nutshell, a complex is an emotionally charged cluster of ideas and feelings within one's unconscious. It became emotionally charged because of the difficulty one had addressing or expressing those emotions at the appropriate times throughout one's life. Like the rings of a tree that build layer upon layer of growth through the years, so too a complex builds emotional power layer upon layer that has never found expression. And with our tree analogy, the core ring, the center stem leading up from the root, Jung tells us, is influenced by an archetype.

Complexes are emotionally laden themes in our life, symptoms of related thoughts and emotions tied together by a psychologically powerful event. They are emotionally charged ideas, memories, and feelings within the unconscious, of which long-forgotten emotional experiences are good examples. In fact, these memories have probably been repressed and remained out of consciousness, undetected and undisturbed, for a long time. Quoting Jung:

> Generally the complexes have to do with unpleasant things which one would rather forget and of which one has no wish to be reminded. The complexes themselves are the result, as a rule, of painful experiences and impressions (Jung, 1954, p. 109).

We become reminded of these emotionally laden memories when they are activated by others' words, actions, or silence. Like a balloon being popped, the complex becomes triggered, and the pent-up emotion bursts forth in a range of power from mild to menacing. Once this complex has been forced to the surface, "constellated," the emotion is released for all to see and can be quite profound, scary, and overwhelming. Not all complexes are intense; some are weak and give us a reflection on our life, or bring a twinge of sadness, regret, or guilt, but they are important to our overall psychological well-being.

> Complexes obviously represent a kind of inferiority in the broadest sense—a statement I must at once qualify by saying that to have complexes does not necessarily indicate inferiority. It only means that something discordant, unassimilated, and antagonistic exists, perhaps as an obstacle, but also as an incentive to greater effort, and so, perhaps, to new possibilities of achievement. In this sense, therefore, complexes are focal or nodal points of psychic life which we would not wish to do without; indeed, they should not be missing, for otherwise psychic activity would come to a fatal standstill. They point to the unresolved problems in the individual, the places where he has suffered a defeat, at least for the time being, and where there is something he cannot evade or overcome—his weak spots in every sense of the word (Jung, 1971, pp. 528-529).

COMPLEX THEORY

Understanding complex theory helps the paranoid individual and the working therapist make sense of many emotions and psychological disorders. This exploration into the unconscious using complex theory is very insightful as a therapeutic tool. For example, one can use the concept of the complex to describe and better understand the emotion of anger, especially explosive anger, that would make no sense using a behavioral or medical model approach.

Suppressed anger, viewed as a complex—each new emotional layer of anger was built upon the previous layers of unresolved anger—grows in strength until constellated, or "sparked" by external events. This anger complex lives dormant in the unconscious until something activates it into consciousness, at which time it can overwhelm the conscious mind, being too emotionally powerful for the ego to handle. An angry person can "blackout" from anger that is too intense; the thoughts are overwhelmed and shut down. It is useful for understanding paranoia and how the individual's life becomes intertwined with paranoia. The complex is always unconscious, for "the ego knows nothing of the existence of numerous psychic complexes." (Jung, 1971, p. 483)

Paranoia behaves and acts like a complex, and can be slowly and properly integrated into the personality only after it has been made conscious—according to the rules of complex theory—and some liberation from paranoia is possible.

Complexes initially come into existence through experiences that resulted in unresolved issues:

- Formidable issues involving love, anxiety, fear, and anger.
- Conflicts that leave one emotionally injured or feeling emotionally incongruent.
- Personal beliefs that were never manifested emotionally.
- Convoluted situations preventing the proper and appropriate emotional release.
- Situations of fear that were not understood or could not be dealt with at that time.

All complexes contain the central theme of fear, anger, anxiety, confusion, or another powerful emotion. During early experiences in life, a child may have experienced something quite emotional, but they could not handle it or had no idea how. This emotional event is associated with archetypal influences, usually connected with the mother or father, or other adults, but since the child was unable to process his emotions (fear, anger, sadness, etc.) at that moment, the complex developed and the child henceforth remained guarded, emotionally repressed, and disturbed by the event.

As the child grew and experienced additional instances of powerful emotions similar to the original experience, the additional emotion *"piled on"* the original experience, and the "cluster of disturbed and hypersensitive emotion" began building. This developing unconscious emotional obstacle—the complex—could not be dealt with by the child because of its intensity and the child's emotional immaturity.

DEVELOPMENT OF THE COMPLEX

At some point in life, an emotional issue takes place that one does not know how to handle, or it is such that one has no control over the situation or the emotional expression necessary to cope effectively with the event at that moment. The unresolved emotional disturbance is repressed by the unconscious mind. Rollo May describes the effect this repression has on the individual:

> Repression and other processes of the blocking off of awareness are in essence methods of ensuring that the usual relation of the past to present will not obtain. Since it would be too painful or in other ways too threatening for the individual to retain certain aspects of his past in this present consciousness, he must carry the past along like a foreign body *in* him but not *of* him, as it were, an encapsulated fifth column which

> thereupon compulsively drives to its out-
> lets in neurotic symptoms (May, 1983, p.
> 138). [In our case, "paranoid symptoms."]

Over time, related emotional issues that cannot be resolved, or are beyond one's ability to handle, are amassed upon this growing complex, and the complex becomes more charged. Often, one forgets what is at the core of this complex and loses insight into why one reacts to similar emotional conflicts. Eventually, this complex becomes quite emotionally primed. Time builds complexes.

Jung makes a point in his writings to note that we probably have thousands of complexes, most of which do not cause us much trouble. Returning to the emotionally charged balloon analogy, complexes initially float within the unconscious without causing much distress. The emotionally charged memory *is* the complex, and as long as it remains unconscious, it does not present trouble; it remains quiet and non-intrusive.

The primary way a memory enters consciousness is by being activated; "something sparked my memory." Some kind of trigger in life provokes this memory and "pops" the balloon—stirring up the central issue of the complex—and once activated, out bursts the emotional energy. This energy takes over one's conscious mind, and one is now under the power of this complex.

Once the powerful, emotionally burdened memory gets activated, the complex is constellated, and one now lives the full force of the complex's attached anxiety or emotion. And activated they will be, be it at home or work, triggered by a person, a certain color, a voice, an object, a place, or an experience. Something triggers the deep, powerful, long-forgotten memory, and one *becomes* the complex—along with all the attached anxiety or emotion.

THE PERSONAL UNCONSCIOUS

While the term "unconscious mind" may describe a part of the human mind, individually, we each have our own personal unconscious mind. Jung says:

> Our experience so far of the nature of unconscious contents permits us, however, to make one general classification. We can distinguish a *personal unconscious*, comprising all the acquisitions of personal life, everything forgotten, repressed, subliminally perceived, thoughts, felt (Jung, 1971, p. 485).

THE ROLE OF THE COMPLEX

Many of our hopes, dreams, fears, stress, regrets, and anxieties elude our conscious mind and are "stored" in the personal unconscious, far from our daily conscious attention. We can pretend that the more negative memories and feelings do not influence our lives, but unconscious does not mean "absent"; out of sight does not mean out of mind. Suppressed and repressed memories of experiences such as trauma, abuse, neglect, and emotionally charged events are stored in our personal unconscious mind for later use. They affect and determine our decisions without us realizing their influence at the moment.

Biological science typically explains that when we eat properly and sleep well, we become physically energized. This energy is ours and is available for us to use as we wish. Our energy expression can be physical, mental, sexual, spiritual, and creative, often directed by our conscious effort. We can put our energies into our muscles to play sports, do physical labor, or exercise. We let this energy move into our brain so we can think, concentrate, worry, use logic to solve problems, ponder our existence, or decide what we want to do next.

We can use this same energy for our sexual expression, creative activities, and outlets. We can stimulate our imagination to invent, create, fantasize, or mentally travel around the world and to distant planets. The moment all our energy ceases, we are probably dead.

Some expression of our energy is with our emotions, feelings, and anxiety (i.e., how we convey our energy with what we are experiencing and with whom we are relating). Anxiety, having its roots in our unconscious mind, directs our energy toward where we feel challenged, and away from what we wish to avoid. We have underlying feelings, often unknown to us at the moment, regarding situations, people, places, and events. In fact, important memories are charged with energy/emotion, ranging from euphoric to destructive and everything in between.

When we remember an event from the past, we also remember its "feeling-tone," and this feeling stays with us longer than the memory associated with it. Thoughts and memories flow through our daily lives, even if we are not consciously paying attention to them. After a long day of thinking about, reflecting upon, and remembering events of our life—especially memories of emotionally provoking events—we can become overcharged with feelings and emotions. Certain memories hold more emotion than others.

The unconscious is playing a role in us at all times. Its influence gives us pause for thought, at times prompting us to do things we later will say, "Why did I do that?" Some of our disturbing long-term memories within our personal unconscious make our decisions extra difficult because they result in confusion, doubt, anxiety, and excessive emotion. At some time or place, we remember and interact with a memory of an event or person, and we become charged with feeling and emotion, with energy.

Being aware of this energy and where it comes from, we have choices. We can reject it, integrate it through understanding, or let it rule our decision-making and behaviors. This is basically how a complex works. Memories are stored in one's personal unconscious mind—mainly those memories which are charged with emotions—ones that are important to us and those associated with major events in our lives. We store these memories along with the associated feelings and emotions. When the memory returns, so do the feelings and emotions.

COMPLEXES AND "MEANING"

To experiment with this idea, try a little exercise and consciously pay attention to your feelings. Sit for a moment and ponder on your past. Let your mind go to the farthest reaches of your memory. Go way, way back. What does it pull up for you? Is it just a neutral memory, innocuous, forgetful? Chances are it is not. Does this memory have meaning and value? What are the powerful feelings and emotions associated with this memory? Most important about this little experiment is that the feeling-tone, which keeps our memories alive and active within the personal unconscious, co-determines the importance of this memory and whether we even keep it as a memory, for without a feeling-tone, this memory would decay. Fuller states:

> Feeling...is involved in the self-formation of all cognitions [memories], sometimes with more, sometimes with less, intensity (Fuller, 1990, p. 210).

Memories are ripe with meaning. They are attached with emotions that give this particular memory its power. Fuller shows that identifying the feelings, not necessarily the memory itself or the object of memory, is what is most important to us.

> When we recall the loss of something of
> some significance to us, it is the loss itself
> that has come to life once again in its
> impact. The loss itself is what is paying us
> a visit and weighing us down, the loss itself
> that we are coming back to and not some
> objective or subjective in-itself (Fuller,
> 1990, p. 269).

And with these memories comes the charge of feelings and emotions. The memory may stay but a moment, but the triggered emotion and feeling linger a lot longer, possibly until those feelings can be consciously addressed. If too many memories surface at a time, one can quickly become overwhelmed with the attached emotions and feelings.

Once a complex is constellated, we must deal with the associated emotion. Complexes can be super-charged and highly energized, asserting their greatest influence and control over us not only in our personal unconscious, but also by disturbing our consciousness. The activated complex dominates our conscious mind and challenges us emotionally, and one is forced to reckon with its power. Addressing this constellation, Jung puts it this way:

> This term simply expresses the fact that the
> outward situation releases a psychic process
> in which certain contents gather together
> and prepare for action. When we say that
> a person is "constellated" we mean that
> he has taken up a position from which he
> can be expected to react in a quite definite
> way. But the constellation is an automatic
> process which happens involuntarily and
> which no one can stop of his own accord.
> The constellated contents are definite com-

plexes possessing their own specific energy
(Jung, 1960/1969, p. 94).

When a life situation occurs that compels a complex to become constellated, one feels the emotional explosion but may have no memory of its origin, or gain insight as to why one is reacting so strongly. For example, with just the sight of a crowd, some people temporarily experience enormous fear where they cannot think clearly, talk coherently, or focus on what is happening to them. What they realize is that they are scared, panicky, and must avoid this place. This person avoids crowds in the future, with no deeper insight as to why.

Some people, at just the mention of the word "father" (or any other trigger word), will become temporarily enraged that they cannot think clearly; they begin threatening others, go "ballistic," yell, and throw things. This anger can last a few minutes or hours. The emotion will eventually settle down but with the possibility of no new understanding of why it occurred.

Jung writes that not only do we have complexes, but that "the complexes have us." Let me clarify that complexes do not always release anger but can elicit a host of various affects. Overwhelming fear, anxiety, worry, love, and behavioral issues can all result from a complex being constellated. Once this complex energy takes over, it is as if one's logic and better judgment have flown out the window. One is now under the emotional control of the complex's power.

ACTIVATED COMPLEXES

A personal example from your own life may be helpful here. Think of a time in your life when you became extremely emotional, so overwhelmed by feelings, anger, anxiety, or confusion (more than the usual amount), and try to recall what sparked that intense upheaval. Was it triggered by the situation you were in, a person's words, a flashback? Was the powerful emotion associated with that trigger? This would be an example of a complex that had been activated.

One's usual everyday anger from situational issues or relationship conflicts can be understandable; we can make sense of our reaction and realize what has gotten us so angry. But sometimes, we are overly angry, furious beyond our usual, above and beyond what we would expect. When a complex gets activated, we lose our usual demeanor and become overly excited, overly fearful, or overly angry. We have temporarily lost our thinking mind and have become pure emotion. The complex is in charge; "the complex has us."

DEWEY

Let me give an example of a man who had a strong complex activated and behaved in a manner that he would otherwise deny was possible. Dewey works as a consultant for an oil and gas company at various work sites around the country. At home, he has a girlfriend he has known for about a year, loves her deeply, provides for her, and passionately looks forward to returning home after a week or two on the road. He was happy with the direction his life was taking and had hopes of proposing marriage soon.

One day, while he was working a couple of states away, he got a phone call from his girlfriend; she told him she was not happy and that she had been fooling around with someone else. She no longer wanted Dewey as her boyfriend.

Dewey says he does not remember what happened to him after that moment, but he learned the next day as reality set back in. Dewey had become enraged. He had walked off his job, got into his truck, and headed home, the whole time texting his girlfriend that he was going to kill her. He had described in gruesome detail what he would do to her once he got his hands on her.

His girlfriend notified the police. When Dewey arrived home, the police were waiting for him; he was arrested and put in jail. He says he "woke up" from his emotional shock the next day and did not know where he was or what he had done. He was told what had transpired, and he had difficulty believing he could have done and said all those things to his now ex-girl-friend. This is an example of a powerful complex that overtook Dewey's consciousness, and he lost his ability to think and reason. He had become (purely, singly, wholly, absolutely, fully) emotional. He became possessed by pure rage.

There is more to this story later in this chapter, but what is being described here is an example of how a powerful complex can take possession of one's consciousness once constellated. Dewey repeatedly stated that he did not know he was capable of acting out in this manner. If this were only a minor complex, one that did not trigger excessive amounts of emotion, he would soon have been able to get himself under control and reflect upon this sudden turn in his relationship. But at the moment the complex was constellated, he was unable to recognize it, and it took his ego out of commission for about a day.

After he returned to "normal," he regretted everything he had said and done, still concerned about why he had "lost it." What caused such an upheaval? What was at the core of this complex? He later realized that his exceedingly strong anger had been triggered by the news of his girlfriend's infidelities, lies, and deceptions but that the deeper source of this complex lay elsewhere, in his past. Do you believe Dewey would have actually killed his girlfriend if he got near enough to her while under the power of the complex?

On par with Siegel using the phrase "the demon of para-noia" as a wonderful description of paranoia's influence, one feels as if one is being taken over by something demonic, some-thing possesses them, something one cannot escape once it has started overtaking them. But if we push the metaphor aside, what we are talking about is the complex. And paranoia acts and behaves like a complex that has been activated.

The constellated complex attaches itself to the personality, overrides the ego with affect and emotion, and one's conscious mind becomes possessed by it. If one's paranoia is minor, the released emotional and affective power will slowly ease from temporary domination over the ego, and one can then go about their daily life without too much suspiciousness, distrust, or need for isolation. After the paranoid feelings subside, one will return to their usual emotional self and will then be able to reflect upon what had happened to them during this temporary takeover by the complex. One will be able to "gather up" the emotion and "stuff it back in," so to speak, and go about life in one's usual normal way. But the longer a complex exists, and the more emotional power it has accumulated, it can become independent of the personality, a complex that now thinks and acts on its own.

AUTONOMOUS COMPLEXES

As long as paranoia does not grow exceedingly strong over the years, one can still get it under control and can function within the bounds of "normal social functioning." But once the complex achieves heightened emotional independence from our ego, becoming ubiquitously active, an ill-tempered powerhouse in the personal unconscious, it is now an *autonomous complex.*

The autonomous complex has successfully separated from the ego-personality and exists independently of the ego and consciousness. Paranoia can be understood, initially, as a minor, temporary, inconvenient way of experiencing fear and suspicion of others, distrust, and one's negative evaluation of oneself. The longer paranoia exists in one's life, and the longer the underlying constituents are not dealt with sufficiently, paranoia can develop to the extreme of becoming a controlling, dominating complex, taking over one's everyday life, possibly permanently.

Some complexes splinter off from one's typical personality and show themselves with great conscious turbulence. Given the length of time and overall control paranoia has usurped in one's life, paranoia initially exists as a "suspicious, on-again/off-again" intrusion in one's life. If it has gained sufficient power, manifesting to an extreme through total isolation, total distrust, and the poorest of low self-esteem, one's paranoia takes on the strength of an autonomous complex. It is now a pervasive suspiciousness, complete distrust, and complete withdrawal and isolation from others. Now, the constellated complex cannot be integrated back into the ego-personality once it has become autonomous. Jung:

> What has happened? Obviously at some time or other the idea of being a persecuted victim gained the upper hand, became autonomous, and formed a second subject which at times completely replaces the healthy ego. It is characteristic that neither of the two subjects can fully experience the other... They know each other intimately, but they have no valid arguments against one another. The healthy ego cannot counter the affectivity of the other, for at least half its affectivity has gone over into its opposite number (Jung, 1960, pp. 227-228).

The autonomous complex has become a "demon," taking total control over one's thinking, feelings, reasoning, beliefs, and individual self. One loses their previous long-identified personal ego through a complete possession by paranoia, as it has now become an independent, always active and functioning, autonomous complex. When one's life is completely overtaken by paranoia as an autonomous complex, one is *possessed* by paranoia all the time.

Using the personal pronoun:

"My paranoia is a complex, at first possibly a minor complex, a little here and there, only once in a while, but if I do not talk about my difficulties, if I am not impelled to work therapeutically on the underlying constituents, paranoia gains power. When I:

1. am alone a lot and do not talk to others about my personal life and feelings…
2. continue to distrust others and stay away from them even if I have no actual supportive evidence to distrust "everyone…"
3. take every negative word that anyone says against me to heart and start believing I really am the negative identity I use against myself…

…then I eventually become more and more distrustful, more lonely, and more negatively self-identified.

I shy away from others more, even peers and family, believing the unknown-other is correct when talking about me and degrading me. I feel negatively judged by others, so why should I hang out with people if they are going to treat me disrespectfully and talk about me behind my back? I don't need them. I do not need anyone, and I withdraw into my own thoughts, my isolation. I allow no one else in and am trapped by my fear, anger, and suspiciousness."

A person with a strong feeling-toned complex is less able to react smoothly…as he is continually hindered and disturbed by the

uncontrollable influences of the complex
(Jung, 1960, p. 45).

If negative thoughts and loneliness are constant with
no break in intensity, paranoia has the increasing potential to
become an autonomous complex, one that is no longer attached
in a healthy way to one's personality. Paranoia can become
another personality—dethroning one's primary ego—achieving
its own autonomy. Paranoia is now a complete and permanent
structure alongside one's original personality.

> The isolated complexes exist side by side
> without any reciprocal influence; they do
> not interact, mutually balancing and cor-
> recting each other. Though firmly knit in
> themselves, with a logical structure, they
> are deprived of the correcting influence
> of complexes with a different orientation.
> Hence it may easily happen that a partic-
> ularly strong and therefore particularly
> isolated and uninfluenceable complex
> becomes an "over-valued idea," a dominant
> that defies all criticism and enjoys complete
> autonomy... (Jung, 1971, p. 277).

The autonomous complex is not one's "true self" as one
may have originally defined oneself, but another personality
that has gotten too strong and has taken over one's life. One has
become dominated by the paranoid complex.

> If the complex does not operate properly,
> either overloaded by its archetypal kernel,
> traumatized by experience or rejected by
> the ego, then the complex will take on a

life of its own, becoming autonomous and pathological (Shalit, 2002, p. 70).

If the paranoid complex becomes autonomous, one is sub-jugated by this complex, and paranoia now exists permanently. One now lives paranoid all the time, around the clock, in all situations encountered in life, and all people are suspect and distrusted.

ARCHETYPAL INFLUENCES

It has already been mentioned that an archetype influences the core or emotional center of a complex, and a clearer explanation here will give further understanding of one's paranoid complex's formation, i.e., what brings paranoia into existence. Jung clearly points out that an archetypal influence is at the core—the nucleus and birthplace of a complex. The word "archetype" is a construct whose meaning is the deep influence that contributes to behavior patterns in human experiences. These patterns are how people live and have lived since the beginning of civiliza-tion and human involvement on earth.

Archetypes have an *a priori* existence, living and having relevance in human lives before we have ever thought about them or their existence. There are many kinds of archetypes,[19] all manifestations of living in various ways. No *person* is an archetype, but we are all made up of these patterns, and no one can lay claim to being a reincarnation of a specific archetype, at least not within a healthy mental state.

Archetypal patterns are bigger than we, mere humans, and they have a greater influence over our lives than we may realize. We are living out these patterns of behavior in our everyday exis-

---

[19] The Great Mother, Wise old man, the hero, savior, trickster, anima, animus, the shadow, the child, Self, the caregiver, the creator, the fool, to name a dozen or so.

tence. Whether conscious of it or not, we are also predisposed to the effects of the archetypes, which are a major influence on our lives by acting from behind the scenes. Archetypes do not belong to us, but we hold their influence in our personal unconscious. An archetypal influence is at the core of complexes, and those particularly connected to paranoia are discussed in greater detail ahead.

During some experiences in life, one may have a powerful memory return, and one becomes so emotionally overwhelmed that the actual memory is consciously blotted out. One is now living out the emotional force of this complex or doing one's best to avoid this emotionally charged experience after it has been constellated.

Since an archetype is at the center of a complex, it must be true that there was a time *before* the complex became the aroused emotional situation and concern in the individual's emotional life, i.e., a time before the complex got "planted." Something had to have happened that the individual experienced as "I can't handle this" or "I don't know what to do." From that moment on, the complex gathers more energy to it, and the healthy, living expression of this archetypal pattern gets buried under all the negative affect.

Eventually, the archetypal influence at the complex's core must be integrated back into the ego-personality, or we risk it becoming autonomous, a separate entity completely detached from the ego. A complex that is attached to the ego is a struggle one hopefully comes to terms with. It is a problem that one will suffer every time one encounters this complex, but aside from feeling its emotional power, one realizes it must be worked on psychologically. One must get through this.

It becomes very disconcerting to deal with these powerful emotions every time a similar situation arises. One may try to avoid these situations and emotions or learn to block them out and run from them, but the complex is still there. It is not going anywhere before it is completely understood and dissolved back into the personality in a healthy way.

As an example of an archetypal influence, let us examine our understanding of the *mother*. Mothers have been around since the beginning of human time, and since no one gets to earth without being born of a mother, the mother archetype is a way of living, a role that most of us understand and have experienced to some degree, whether or not we have ever been an actual mother.

We are not talking about the personal mother here when we talk about this archetype. The human mother is a female heavily influenced by this archetypal energy, but she is still a human, not an archetype. The archetype of the mother has been shaped through all the ages and cultures that have imbued "mother" with meaning. This archetype is the procreative influence, the mother of the divine, the vessel that gives birth to humans and gods alike. But a mother is so much more than this. Jung gives us a description of the mother archetype, which provides us with a depth of understanding as to what it means to be "mother," not just in the present, but throughout the history of motherhood: the feelings, the comfort, the negative aspects, and the generalities. I am quoting from his paper "Psychological Aspects of the Mother Archetype":

> The qualities associated with it are maternal solicitude and sympathy; the magic authority of the female; the wisdom and spiritual exaltation that transcend reason; and helpful instinct or impulse; all that is benign, all that cherishes and sustains, that fosters growth and fertility. The place of magic transformation and rebirth, together with the underworld and its inhabitants, are presided over by the mother. On the negative side the mother archetype may

connote anything secret, hidden, dark;
the abyss, the world of the dead, anything
that devours, seduces, and poisons, that
is terrifying and inescapable like fate. ...
Although the figure of the mother as it
appears in folklore is more or less universal, this image changes markedly when it
appears in the individual psyche. ...That is
to say, all those influences which the literature describes as being exerted on the children do not come from the mother herself,
but rather from the archetype projected
upon her, which gives her a mythological
background and invests her with authority
and numinosity (Jung, 1959, pp. 81-83).

What Jung has done is open up and broaden our understanding of what "mother" means to include all time and history,
within religion, mythology, and folklore. This is what archetypes
are, patterns of human behavior and achievement throughout
history, into and from the depth of human experience.

Presenting a similar discourse on the archetypal aspects of
father, we find:

"The fathers" are the representatives of
law and order, from the earliest taboos to
the most modern juridical systems; they
hand down the highest values of civiliza-
tion. ...The world of the fathers is thus the
world of collective values; it is historical
and related to the fluctuating level of conscious and cultural development within the
group. The prevailing system of cultural
values, i.e., the canon of values which gives
a culture its peculiar physiognomy and its

stability, has its roots in the fathers, the grown men who represent and reinforce the religious, ethical, political, and social structure of the collective.

These fathers are the guardians of masculinity and the supervisors of all education. That is to say, their existence is not merely symbolical; as pillars of the institutions that embody the cultural canon, they preside over the upbringing of each individual and certify his coming of age. It makes no difference how this cultural canon is constituted, whether its laws and taboos be those of a tribe of head-hunters or of a Christian nation. Always the fathers see to it that the current values are impressed upon the young people, and that only those who have identified themselves with those values are included among the adults. The advocacy of the canon of values inherited from the fathers and enforced by education manifests itself in the psychic structure of the individual as "conscience" (Neumann, 1954, pp. 172-173).

The preceding descriptions of mother and father describe the archetypal influences as they manifest through the actual human mother or father. But the mother archetype and father archetype are not always positive. There is always the negative, the "dark side" that cannot be ignored for the safety of children and all humanity.

Some negative aspects of the mother archetype are her desire to control, nag, and torment emotionally. She is known to dominate her children and husband, restrict, bitch, devour, limit, deny, and demand. She is known for her infidelities and her ability to smother her children, kill them, and all the behaviors we find in children's stories, mythology, and even in the daily evening news.

We can open our eyes and witness the negative aspects of the mother archetype living through the lives of humans, and although a difficult concept to understand, the mother archetype can also be lived out through the masculine. A man can become "possessed" by the negative mother archetype, and he will then live out her influences through his masculine weakness, by his negative and controlling ways.

Likewise, the father archetype has a negative dark side, namely his desire to dominate and control, abuse, restrict, limit, deny, forbid, remain childish, destroy creativity, rape, ignore, and abandon. He has been known for his infidelities and his desire to abandon his children to the world of only the feminine, avoid his responsibilities to his wife and children, and he is guilty of all the behaviors we see in children's stories, mythology, religion, legends, and everyday actions of negative, insensitive, and irresponsible men.[20] Again, the evening news is filled with examples of the worst of men's actions and behaviors.

Starting early in life, we develop an image in our mind of what an ideal father or mother should be. Through childhood, we observe others' parents, fathers, and mothers in society, how parents are portrayed on television, and our imagination develops an image of what a "perfect" mother and father should be for us. This "ideal" parent that we have imaginatively developed, and the influences of the archetypal "perfect" parent, begin affecting our thinking and beliefs.

If one is influenced by religion, the idea of God as Father and other masculine and feminine divine beings can become incorporated into our image of the ideal. Then, based on this

---

[20] For examples of the negative mother or father in action, see the writings of Hans Christian Andersen, Aesop, the Bible, Greek mythology, and nursery rhymes.

imaginative ideal, we develop our belief of what a mother "should be," what a father "should be," and how each of them should act.

> Besides his personal father there is a "higher," that is to say an archetypal, father figure, and similarly an archetypal mother figure appears beside the personal mother (Neumann, 1954, p. 132).

We look at our real biological, human parents, and we find flaws. We see who we really have in reality, and often they do not measure up to our imaginative ideal. There is a big difference between the two, the human and the imagined parent.

Humans are not archetypes, but we do live out the influences and patterns of the archetypes. It is through the living-out of these archetypal influences that we experience either satisfaction or conflict. When young, we are at the mercy of our biological parents, who are influenced by archetypal patterns, some healthy, some not-so-healthy. If a child's parents are good people, sensitive, caring, and adequate, they may not get out of childhood "unscathed;" they may not have the seeds of paranoia planted.

As is true in the development of paranoia, we find a child who is confronted by archetypal energy where they have no knowledge or experience with which to cope, and they begin suffering emotionally. If this negative impact on their life continues without abatement, then the "kernel" of paranoia has been sown. But negative archetypal energy is not the only influence needed to create paranoia. One's ongoing lifestyle also determines whether paranoia takes root. The other influences we have identified are loneliness, low self-esteem, and distrust. All these factors must come together compositionally for paranoia to manifest as a part of the personality.

Feminine and masculine lifestyles are lived out in many forms and have been throughout the ages. Each generation is influenced by previous generations. Our parents were influenced by their parents and grandparents, and so on, back through time. When it is said that archetypal influences are at the core of a complex, one usually looks at the negative aspects of the masculine or feminine caretakers and other influential adults to see what those influences were, how they put the child into difficult, uncompromising, and inescapable situations.

It would be better, instead of only looking at and blaming the actual fallible human who acquired the title "mother" or "father," that we examine the archetypal influences that were dominant and controlling, that set up opportunities for the child to be psychologically, emotionally or physically abused, ignored, or unaccepted, placing upon them excessive and unattainable demands. The child was put into situations where they could not succeed because of immaturity, lack of emotional strength, or the impossibility of actual human or universal laws.

The following are a few examples that may lead to a better understanding of the destructive influence negative archetype patterns can have on young people.

FOUR STORIES OF ARCHETYPAL INFLUENCES

Tony was five years old when his mother began sending him outside in the hot or cold, rainy or sunny weather. It did not matter. She put him out so she could "entertain" men. Tony started hating his mother. He knew she was cheating on his father. He was warned and threatened by his mother not to tell anyone of her dalliances over the years. He grew to distrust women, and since he never spoke of this to others, he kept his thoughts, feelings, and body to himself, feeling alone and separated from others because of what he knew, the "secret" he could not talk about.

The negative archetypal patterns that Tony continues to deal with are cruelty, abandonment, distrust, lies, and deception, to name just a few. He now sees the world through paranoid eyes. Tony says he can no longer trust anyone, stays isolated, and has a low opinion of himself.

George was tortured and abused by his father daily when he was young, and his mother ignored what was happening. He was too scared to tell anyone and was threatened with more abuse if he did. He would dissociate just to get through the abuse. The marks left on his body were hidden by his clothing. George developed a strong hate for his father that continues to this day, years after his father's death. He believed he had been abandoned by the world, that no one cared about him, and that he always had to be self-protective.

To this day, he trusts no one, lives alone as far out in the woods as he can, and avoids relationships. He says that the memories of his father and the abuse are triggered by sounds, smells, sights, tastes, and certain words. When triggered, he flies into a rage, hurts people, and has been arrested many times. He hates men, but can tolerate women. Archetypally, George struggled with the threat of physical harm, torture, violence, sexual abuse, helplessness, abandonment, distrust in elders, and other uncompromising situations. George knows he is paranoid and only reluctantly talks about it with his therapist. He says it mystifies him that he can trust his therapist but admits that his therapist is the only person on earth with whom he has been able to build trust.

Jerri witnessed her father being taken from her by the law. Her mother often accused her father of domestic abuse without evidence, and her mother could be quite convincing. Jerri loved her father very much and knew what her mother was doing. Jerri had to grow up without her father since he eventually got tired of being accused wrongfully and being put in jail. On the other hand, her mother was a mean-spirited, vindictive woman who enjoyed the company of abusive men outside of her marriage, which led to Jerri being put in situations to be abused by these men.

She grew to distrust both men and women, but she hated her mother for what, as a nine-year-old child, she saw her mother do to her father; that mother was responsible for her father's incarcerations and eventual abandonment of Jerri. She believed her mother had provoked her father so she could live out her infidelities. Jerri faced abandonment, physical and sexual abuse, and being put in uncompromising situations, to name a few of the difficult archetypal patterns she would have to face alone.

Growing up, Jerri never got along with her mother, with constant tension, hate, and distrust between them. She developed low self-esteem related to abandonment, her parents fighting, and the sexual abuse from men that her mother brought home. Jerri continues to be very suspicious of both men and women, distrusts "all" people, and hasn't been able to maintain personal relationships for more than a few months at a time. She is slowly realizing why she is paranoid.

As we continue with Peter's personal story from previous chapters, he hates his father for abandoning the family after his parents' divorce. Peter grew up without his father, and felt inadequate, not like the other boys. He saw other boys with their fathers, realizing how lonely he felt. Whenever he saw his father in public, his father did not acknowledge his son and went about his own business, leaving Peter angry, lonely, and feeling abandoned over and over again.

Throughout his childhood, Peter attempted to get attached to other boys' fathers so he could "feel like I fit in," but he knew he was an outsider. He learned he did not and could not trust men. He felt very insecure as a boy, and now, as a developing young man, he realizes he has never had an actual strong male role model to teach him what he needs to know; how to be a man.

When he goes out in public, he believes everyone is looking at him and judging him negatively as "a bastard" (the voice of the unknown-other), as if they know he has no father. Peter struggles with abandonment to only feminine influence, lack of a male role model, being an outsider, plus other archetypal patterns.

These examples, if experienced by anyone else, may never have planted seeds for paranoia. But with these individuals, the negative archetypal influences conflicted with the "ideal" of mother or father within the child, and anger and distrust were generated. The lived-experiences were enough for these individuals to isolate themselves from others in a self-protective, lonely way and view themselves through a negative self-image. They began distrusting others and developing paranoia.

These experiences for these individuals did not plant seeds of approval, belonging, relationship-building, contentment, personal satisfaction, and emotional strength, but instead, distrust, anger, low self-esteem, hate, loneliness: *paranoia*. The paranoid individual will tell you which parent they are most angry at and distrusts the most, but they may not be able to explain the archetypal pattern they could not deal with emotionally.

Here I'd like to return to the earlier story in this chapter involving the man named Dewey who, while working a couple of hundred miles from home, set out to kill his girlfriend after she broke up with him. After his arrest, he was told by the judge he had to get psychological therapy. Dewey agreed and wanted to better understand how he could lose all control of himself and threaten to kill his girlfriend—not part of his usually mild nature.

This was not the only breakup he has had but was similar to others he's had in the past, all of which affected him emotionally. Four years earlier, he and his wife divorced, and in therapy, he discovered that he was still very bitter about that. Initially, he thought everything in that marriage was good, but he discovered that his wife was cheating on him. It devastated him at that time, but he did not talk about it then; he suppressed his anger and moved on in life toward another relationship.

With further therapy, Dewey rediscovered deep anger toward his father for cheating on his mother, and his father's responsibility for the breakup of his parents' marriage. Dewey says he had never talked about these previous breakups and the destruction of marriages, but they were all related to infidelity. He now believed that the dissolution of his parents' marriage so negatively affected him as a child that he was very sensitive to whom he could trust. He placed a great deal on the importance of being able to trust someone and any lie or deception disturbed him greatly.

This anger and distrust had been building up in him for many years before this most recent relationship breakup. He now believes that this intended attack on his girlfriend was an accumulating result of many years of unresolved anger. He realized that the previous emotional conflicts closely related at the core became too much for him and overwhelmed his ego, and the complex took charge.

He wondered how he could have been so blind to the infidelities of his chosen mates over the years, similar to the infidelity pattern he witnessed in his father. This was not a minor complex but a fully charged, emotionally powerful one that, once constellated, took over his logical-thinking brain. Only his pure anger, hate, and rage surfaced; he became possessed by this complex.

SUMMARY

Complexes are always unconscious, and when activated, the feeling-tone or associated emotions begin acting upon us consciously. Others can trigger complexes by what they say and do, or by their behavior toward us. They can be triggered by an event closely associated with original, possibly long-forgotten experiences that initially set the complex in place. A word, an action, a sight, a memory, or a person's furtive glance can all activate and constellate a complex into consciousness.

Upon constellation, one can realize the existence of this complex if one is psychologically interested and astute enough to pay attention. In an average psychologically healthy person with a large variety of complexes, through psychotherapy, there comes the opportunity to integrate these complexes and the attached feelings into one's personality and become psychologically strengthened. One can awaken to forgotten and unconscious aspects of the personality, acknowledge the power in a complex, and help oneself add to their conscious wholeness—their individuality.

We each are responsible for delving into our paranoia and discussing its roots; no one else can do it for us. We need to discover what or who, archetypally, is behind our paranoia, i.e., what are the original roots that continue to support our paranoid outlook on life? We can, with effort, discover the archetypal core that took hold of our inadequacy and vulnerability. Take the time to explore these roots. Pull them up so they can be talked about and dealt with more effectively and productively.

Paranoia makes for a difficult life and does not produce good relationships. It isolates one individual from another. Integrating the complexes into an ever-expanding conscious personality allows one to move along their path of "individuation."

THERAPEUTIC DIALOGUE

W ORKING WITH PARANOID CLIENTS HAS its challenges. What these clients need in therapy is a therapist who understands paranoia in its essence. One who will work alongside them through the therapeutic maelstrom, helping them understand what they experience and providing some way through the loneliness, distrust, and self-persecution that currently dominates their lives. Additionally, they need help to deal with their fear, anxiety, anger, and social limitations. This sounds like typical therapeutic work; it is, but with our focus on the essence of paranoia, we now have a clearer understanding of what our paranoid clients are experiencing, even if they initially cannot verbalize it.

Can we help our clients trust again, even if they could trust no one for years? Can we redirect our clients away from negative self-judgment and toward more positive self-esteem? Is there a cure for loneliness, a way to improve their interpersonal relationships? There are no pills to cure paranoia, no computer software, no pencil tests, or question/answer forms that will help our client stop being paranoid. A long road of talking and therapeutic intervention is ahead if our clients hope to understand the impact paranoia has had on their lives and possibly learn to work with the roots of paranoia to better their lives.

If we, the therapist, can use our client's paranoia as a guide to deeper and more meaningful dialogue, we will hear the "important stuff" that has gone into making them so paranoid. We will hear the disturbances, anger, fear, distrust, loneliness, and isolation. It may be possible to help our paranoid clients move away from a lifestyle plagued by paranoia.

One just does not "have" paranoia, like a label or sticker one displays on one's forehead. One *is* paranoid. Each paranoid individual *is* paranoid to some degree, and the individual degree of paranoia affects and influences all aspects of their life. It is also not something one can just "get over"; one must work through all underlying aspects of paranoia, including other difficult idiosyncrasies of one's life, before one may even notice a decrease in paranoid symptoms.

This chapter addresses therapeutic issues for the therapist who works with paranoid clients. The therapist should be able to recognize paranoia in their client more easily and understand the structure of paranoia and how it manifests in life, i.e., what makes paranoia what it is. In fact, the therapist will use all their usual philosophical- and psychological-orientation tools to help their paranoid client, but now with a focus on what governed this client toward the paranoid lifestyle and how to address those personal issues in therapy.

Paranoia can often be one of many problems our clients struggle within their troubled lives. The major benefit of using a phenomenological study such as this is that when we understand the psychological constituents of paranoia, we recognize those constituents in our clients and are assured that we are dealing with paranoia. We now have a guide on how to proceed with therapy.

Our clients are likely to have other personality and emotional disorders. We may also be dealing with social anxiety, bipolar disorder, addiction, phobias, schizophrenia, generalized anxiety disorder, explosive anger disorder, and depression. Of course, these mental, emotional, personality disorders, and life struggles need to be addressed, but paranoia now stands out as also an important, underlying, controlling, ongoing roadblock to this person's relationships, emotional development, mental health, individuation, and future.

THE THERAPIST

One of the first things a therapist must do is take care of themself. The therapist must be psychologically secure in their own life to deal with the mental illnesses of others. It is a strong suggestion, and some would say psychologically required, that the mental health therapist has many hours of their own personal therapy with a thoughtful, thorough, and skillfully advanced analyst. The therapist must be mentally and emotionally prepared to work in all kinds of settings, with many types of people, with a multitude of emotional and mental illnesses.

Transference and countertransference issues will always present themselves, and the therapist must have the knowledge and means to address them. Having gone through their own emotional issues in therapy gives the therapist inner strength and an approach to mental illness that can support them during tough times with their client. Jung (Jung, 1954/1966) writes:

> ...we have to defend ourselves against the same influences to which our patients have succumbed. Like doctors who treat epidemic diseases, we expose ourselves to powers that threaten our conscious equilibrium, and we have to take every possible precaution if we want to rescue not only our own humanity but that of the patient... (p. 79).

> In other words, the art of psychotherapy requires that the therapist be in possession of avowable, credible, and defensible convictions which have proved their viability either by having resolved any neurotic dissociations of his own or by preventing them from arising. A therapist with a neurosis is a contradiction in terms. One cannot help any patient to advance further than one has advanced oneself (p. 78).

The therapist must have enough education and access to pre-existing knowledge and research of every psychological and life problem their clients may bring to the session. Psychology is always strengthening in understanding human suffering, and the therapist needs to keep pace with all advances in knowledge and methods of psychological work.

Establish Boundaries

It is very important to establish clear boundaries with our paranoid clients. Issues of confidentiality and boundaries may need to be discussed often in therapy. Remember, these clients do not trust you or your intent to help them. They will become suspicious of the questions you ask and want to know if you have underlying motives when you ask these questions. Be very clear about no contact or communication with clients outside the therapy office. The therapist may need to explain the ethical code of behavior between therapist and client, and how this code helps to build trust.

One therapist told me of a client who accused him of being the dark figure standing in the corner of this client's living room who talks to him and questions his thoughts and actions. This man lives in a dark room, always fearful of who is outside, ready to break in on him and take advantage of him. He was visually projecting the unknown-other, and he believed it was his therapist who was standing there in his room because of the wording of the questions being asked.

If the paranoid person fears your questions or feels you are spying and snooping into his personal life, they may not return for their next appointment out of fear of being too exposed. Their paranoia will tell them that this "therapeutic relationship" is threatening, just like "all other relationships I've ever had." We must wait for them to open up and talk about their life's conflicts. We cannot go there uninvited. We must tread respectfully with our questions, so the paranoid client does not feel invaded or exposed. Slow is better.

If the therapist cannot respect the paranoid client's need for patience and allow them to open themself up slowly to questions, or if the therapist reacts too personally to what the client says or how they behave, there may be some countertransference issues that need to be confronted in the therapist.

> It is just common sense to recognize that, in therapy or out, getting along with paranoid individuals means giving them little or nothing to be paranoid about. …A therapist attempting to build basic trust should be particularly on the alert not to upset the patient with threatening actions of a nonverbal sort. It is always wise to set the therapeutic stage in a way and place that reassures both therapist and patient that both are safe. …The therapist should be clear from the start about what the patient can expect from the therapeutic relationship. That way, unpleasant surprises can be avoided (Kantor, 2004, pp. 164-165).

ESTABLISH RAPPORT

One primary requirement of the therapist is to establish rapport and build trust. If you move too quickly and have not developed enough trust, they will look at you as another outside persecutor. Trusting is very difficult for paranoid individuals, and the development of a trustful relationship will probably take a very long time, if ever. They rarely believe in its existence. How can we expect paranoid people to speak openly about their personal fears, weaknesses, and vulnerabilities if they do not trust us? It certainly will test our patience and honesty in wanting to work with paranoid individuals. The slow, necessary development of a trusting relationship may help these clients gain some strength in other relationships and aid them in confronting their inner delusions and torments.

THERAPEUTIC AIMS

We have not invented a new definition of paranoia, but we now have a clearer understanding of the true meaning of paranoia in its constitutive forms. With this better working knowledge of paranoia, how can we use it in therapy?

Therapy can be a long, arduous process, an ongoing dialogue between therapist and client, where the client talks about their life, the therapist listens, and hopefully, together, new insights and better decisions can be made by the client. But who knows best what the client needs, the client or the therapist?

The principal topic of conversation in therapy should be the client's life, and since paranoia is our primary subject here, the question will be: "Is my client paranoid, and how do I address their paranoia?"

The therapist does not go into a therapy session believing they know what is best for the client or that they have all the answers. Regarding the therapeutic relationship between client and therapist, Jung has said:

> As far as possible I let pure experience decide the therapeutic aims. This may perhaps seem strange, because it is commonly supposed that the therapist has an aim. But in psychotherapy it seems to me positively advisable for the doctor not to have too fixed an aim. He can hardly know better than the nature and will to live of the patient. The great decisions in human life usually have far more to do with the instincts and other mysterious unconscious factors than with conscious will and well-meaning reasonableness. The shoe that fits one person pinches another; there is no universal recipe for living. Each of us carries his own life-form within him—an irrational form which no other can outbid (Jung, 1954/1966, p. 41).

The therapist knows what paranoia is, but they certainly do not know how or why this person sitting in front of them became paranoid. That is the discovery for both the client and therapist. How did this person come to feel so lonely? How did they come to distrust so much? Why do they treat themself so negatively and talk about themself with so much contempt and negative self-judgment?

Do you believe the client knows what they need but just cannot get to it on their own? Should the therapist instruct or manipulate the client's thinking so that they can "get over" being paranoid and just become trusting of others? Paranoia developed as a defense, an unconscious attempt to find the help and protection they needed through difficult life situations. Their sense of who they were, their autonomy, had to be protected. It may not have been their conscious intention to protect autonomy and emotional stability, but paranoia became their "best attempt" at maintaining mental footing through very difficult situations. It continues to be their ongoing expression of their need to cope with their intolerable world and their apprehension of maintaining their mental health "center."

If the paranoid client only gets one thing from therapy, it is important that they find trust. If trust for only one other person—you, the therapist—is successful, that is tremendous growth and opportunity for this person who could not trust before. Maybe even for a short while, they may not feel so lonely. Someone has accepted them just as they are.

THERAPEUTIC ALLIANCE

Meissner describes the therapeutic alliance, which is essential for the paranoid client, and how their lack of trust can threaten this coherence.

> While the therapeutic alliance is the *sine qua non* for any effective therapy, and the establishing and maintaining of a therapeutic union must be a matter of high priority—not only at the beginning of the therapeutic process but throughout its full extent—it is obvious that with paranoid patients the therapeutic alliance is placed in considerable jeopardy. The major impediments to the therapeutic alliance are the patient's lack of capacity for trust and the precarious state of the patient's autonomy, both of which are essential ingredients in the evolution of a meaningful therapeutic alliance.

Despite the obvious difficulties and the inherent precariousness of any therapeutic alliance with paranoid patients, the case is not hopeless. With most paranoid patients, the therapist immediately encounters a façade of suspiciousness, guardedness, and secretiveness. While the patient's defenses may be in a state of hypermobilization due to the circumstances which may have brought him to therapy and because of the inherent threats posed by the threatening relationship to the therapist, it is important to remember that the paranoid patient who comes into psychotherapy is there because his paranoia is failing him (Meissner, 1986, pp. 232-233).

Within the safe walls of the therapy office, the therapist is in the position to be the only "friend" this person may have. This temenos is of such importance—possibly the only safe place to find trust and fellowship—that they will protect their personal life and shut you out if sufficient trust has not been built.

The first difficulty is the apparent lack of trust. This is a pervasive problem for all paranoid patients and is more severe in those patients in whom the paranoid manifestations come to dominate the clinical picture. Suspiciousness and an inherent lack of trust become the hallmarks of paranoid psychopathology. Consequently, the issues of lack of trust and the impediments it creates to meaningful psychotherapeutic work must become issues of the highest priority in approaching the treatment of these patients (Meissner, 1986, p. 229).

As the therapist already knows, you cannot be a typical "friend," but you can be open, thoughtful, understanding, sympathetic, and receptive to all the client says. Throughout the trust-building, the paranoid client may realize that at least they are not always alone, not always lonely. Someone is listening to them. Someone understands them. May brings up this topic:

> The acceptance by another person, such as the therapist, shows the patient that he no longer needs to fight his main battle on the front of whether anyone else, or the world, can accept him; the acceptance *frees* him to experience his own being (May, 1983, pp. 101-102).

The therapist becomes that person they can now count on, expect honesty, and hold them accountable for honesty in return. Honesty is a two-way street that supports the foundation of trust. As the therapist, the usual methods and techniques you typically use regarding trust issues with any client would apply here with the paranoid client as well.

I have found that attempts at humor, or the occasional observation made in a joking manner, are not appreciated by the paranoid client. They will wonder what you *really* mean by this display of humor, whether you are trying to insult them, deceive them in some way, or make fun of them just like the voice of the unknown-other does. The voice of the unknown-other will outweigh your sense of humor.

The paranoid client feels the need to protect themself from you and others, so while they are being "who they normally are," they will look at you with suspicion and contempt. Your actions are suspect. For example, there was a therapist who crossed one of their legs over the other, and the client thought they were making advances toward them. We must remember that this person does not trust you any more than they trust anyone, possibly less, because a therapist asks personal questions and digs into one's personal life.

AFFIRMATIVE APPROACH

Therapists who understand paranoia—not as suspiciousness of those "out there" or as just another form of "mental illness"—will recognize the roots, the constituents involved in the paranoid life and help their clients attend to those life issues. We slowly work to undermine paranoia at its foundation. Once rapport has been established and trust built as much as is capable, therapy can continue in its many forms. I believe Kantor is correct when he discusses the importance of taking an affirmative approach with the paranoid client as they sit in your office. Kantor encourages the proactive, accepting approach by:

> Simply agreeing to see the patient... Offering regular therapeutic sessions... Offering positive feedback... Offering a corrective emotional experience... Relieving the low self-esteem that is characteristically found in paranoid individuals (Kantor, 2004, pp. 160-161).

This approach is similar to what Carl Rogers calls "client-centered therapy." The sensitive, feeling, being-there approach gives paranoid clients the confidence to speak about their emotional conflicts, the distance they feel from others, and their isolation.

With a therapist who employs a more confrontational approach, paranoid people may get frustrated, easily annoyed, scared, and they may take what the therapist says sensitively, possibly deciding not to risk their personal life and low self-esteem to scrutiny. With a confrontational approach, again, the therapist becomes another "voice of the unknown-other" that angers and scares the client. This should be avoided; it already matches the voice they use toward themself.

RECOGNIZING THE SIGNS OF PARANOIA

During the early interview process, the therapist may not initially recognize paranoia. It can be well hidden behind the client's fear, anger, anxiety, relationship turmoil, depression, and other emotional disturbances. The therapist may want to pose three questions to the client if paranoia is suspected.

1. How much time do you spend by yourself?
2. Do you trust most people?
3. If you get angry at yourself, how do you treat yourself?

During this interview process, the therapist elicits the client's thoughts and feelings about themself, their self-confidence and self-esteem, their ability to trust others, and how much time they spend alone. The therapist should ask these questions "matter-of-factly" so as not to raise the client's suspicious nature if they are indeed paranoid. If the client fits for these three personal struggles, then the therapist realizes at least one direction they will need to take in this client's therapy.

SYMPTOMS OF PARANOIA

As is common with most clients in therapy, whether outwardly manifested or held tightly closed off from outward expression, anxiety is one of life's core issues that needs attention from the beginning. Whether the client knows the words necessary to describe it, even if they are unaware of it, anxiety manifests in many aspects of their life. If the therapist asks the client what concerns them the most and they describe anxiety symptoms, the therapist questions further to find sources of the anxiety.

Anxiety is a pre-existing condition alongside paranoia, not a cause. All people have some manifestation of anxiety. We know anxiety is an important but often detrimentally dominant aspect of our client's life, and when the therapist asks what creates so much anxiety in their life, they will usually get the answer, "I don't know." Anxiety is always unknown consciously, but originates in their world and from their unconscious mind.

The therapist must be dutiful to recognize the difference between anxiety and paranoia. Anxiety may be in total control of one's thinking and decision-making process, but paranoia may be hiding behind the symptoms of anxiety.

As we listen to our paranoid clients, we may hear how lonely they are. They may also be isolating themselves. How did this person become so lonely and isolated? This is not the same kind of isolation sought by spiritual seekers, such as hermits, nuns, or Buddhists. For the paranoid individual, isolation is harmful, absent of human warmth and contact. It is the isolation that negatively affects one's mind. How might we expand our client's horizons now to include other people? This is not an unusual complaint from many of our non-paranoid clients as well, so whatever usual methods and techniques the therapist uses to deal with loneliness would apply here to the paranoid client.

We will also discover that our paranoid client has low self-esteem, believes no one wants to be around them, and that others talk negatively about them. In fact, the voice of the unknown-other tells them daily: "No one wants you around because you are such a lowlife," as one such client described their intralocution. How do you help this client improve their self-esteem? How do you help them improve the areas of their life they perceive as negative and build confidence to make changes?

Branden addresses the importance of the positive therapeutic attitude when addressing self-esteem issues, stating:

> As with parents and teachers, an unrelent-
> ing attitude of acceptance and respect is
> perhaps the first way in which a psycho-
> therapist can contribute to the self-esteem
> of a client. It is the foundation of useful
> therapy (Branden, 1994, p. 259).

The therapist should already have the necessary tools
in place to help their clients with low self-esteem issues. Low
self-esteem is a typical problem encountered during the therapeutic hour that emerges not only with the paranoid client, but
with clients in general. Just another important day in the office.
Kantor encourages us to help our paranoid client by:

> Relieving the low self-esteem that is char-
> acteristically found in paranoid individuals.
> This low self-esteem is both the cause and
> the product of the paranoid individual's
> sensitivity and vulnerability to criticism,
> humiliation, and rejection, and leads to one
> of the worst problems paranoid patients
> have. ...Relief comes not only from deter-
> mining and isolating the early experiences
> that have left the patient feeling put down,
> but also from offering the paranoid indi-
> vidual a direct antidote in the form of a
> new, expert, professional reassessment of
> the patient's true personal worth. Enhanced
> self-esteem in turn leads to progressively
> developing self-confidence, increased by
> real personal and professional successes,
> however small to start, that have in turn

become possible because of the patient's
enhanced self-pride and newly developing
willingness to take emotional and practical
chances (Kantor, 2004, p. 161).

TECHNIQUE FOR SUSPICION

During therapy sessions with paranoid clients and those who
are suspicious, I have used the following technique to grasp
better what the client struggles with when they distrust and
are suspicious about interacting with others. I have found this
technique useful to open the client to talk about their thoughts
and feelings, of which they are often silent and not consciously
aware.

Whenever a client believes another is acutely observing
their actions, or when they believe they are being criticized and
belittled by others who may or may not be seen, i.e., "people in
general," I ask them what they hear and what they believe others
are saying about them. When the client speaks about worries
and fears of others staring at and talking about them, and if the
client is afraid to be around other people for these reasons, I
usually ask something like this: "When these people are staring
at you, thinking terrible things about you, or talking about you
all the time behind your back, tell me what they are saying."

I am actually asking them what the voice of the unknown-
other is saying about them. With the client's response, I get
a good sense of what they think and feel about themself, but
does not yet understand about themself. When they think others are looking at them, observing their every move, and that
they are being monitored as if under a magnifying lens, I ask
them, "When these people are looking at you, observing you,
and have you under their watchful eye, what must they be saying about you? Tell me the exact words you hear them say when
they describe you as they see you."

This will be difficult for clients because it exposes them; it embarrasses them to disclose such personal information. The client's response *is* the voice of *the unknown-other*, the voice that taunts, persecutes, threatens, and demeans, and the client's response *is* the unacknowledged, unrelenting, undisclosed, and unacceptable aspects of their self-beliefs that are not consciously recognized by them yet—their paranoid thinking. These words, that the client is thinking, express how they feel and what they believe about themself, and they are usually unacknowledged self-condemnation.

Once the client verbalizes their negativity, which they do not like or approve of, it is out in the open, disclosed in the therapy session, and we can now talk about it and work on their self-esteem issues. But if this "unspoken" belief is pointed out to the client as their own inner voice, they will say, "I don't believe it. It really is other people saying those things, not me."

They may deny that they say these things to and about themself, that they strongly believe it is what the "other" is indeed saying and thinking about them. An important therapeutic adage is not to tell the client directly that their thinking is the voice of the unknown-other, but to lead them to discover it for themself. If you enlighten them too directly, the client may not believe that their intralocution is the voice of the unknown-other. They may think you are lying to them, attacking them, or making fun of them. But upon the self-discovery that their intralocution and the voice of the unknown-other match, they may think deeply about these thoughts and pay more attention to their intralocution, especially as they feel negatively influenced by others.

Often our client does not realize or even initially believe that they say these negative things about themself. There is a disconnect between what they think and how they feel, so we will want to help them explore how these put-downs from the unknown-other fit their beliefs about their life. How did their low self-esteem and self-opinion come to exist, and how pervasive is it? Since we can now hear clearly what the voice of the unknown-other is saying, we have the opportunity to help them examine and evaluate their beliefs about themself.

A client may finally admit, "I know, I recognize it now," when prior to that moment, recognizing the voice of the unknown-other as their own intralocution was under the threshold of conscious awareness and understanding. Be careful of the emotions this may now generate. When the client admits to finally hearing themself refer to themself in negative terms, fear and anger may become quite palpable. The client may not initially admit their fear to you, but the fear that was hiding behind their paranoid symptoms is now exposed and needs to be addressed. They may be embarrassed and feel vulnerable because of their exposure.

As was discussed in a previous chapter, the client may become quite angry at themself for how they have been treating themself. The anger and fear are mixed, intertwined, and confused. Now we must take the time to address these emotional issues.

CLIENT-THERAPIST DIALOGUE

Here is an example of what a session may sound like when a client finally realizes who is saying the words of condescension they hear. When they tell you that others talk about them or they are afraid to be around people because they stare and think bad things about them, you may ask them to tell you what others are saying and thinking about them.

Client: When I walk into that store, everyone stares at me. I don't know any of them, but I know they are judging me and talking about me.
Therapist: You know the people in that store are talking about you. Tell me what they might say about you. Tell me the exact words they would use.

Client: They say, "He's stupid, ugly, weird, look at his hair, his clothes don't even fit him right. Look how fat he is."

Therapist: You believe these people are judging you. What else might they be saying about you? Since you believe these people are really judging you, what do they judge about you?

Client: They say things about how shy and lonely I am. They think I'm a pervert. They don't know anything about me. They don't know me, but they judge me anyway.

I encourage you, as their therapist, to have the client state the exact words they hear from the unknown-other, so you are clearly grasping your client's deep, unacknowledged fears and low self-esteem, not some general ideas or vague worries. With the specific words they hear from the unknown-other—actually their intralocution—you can then help them identify what their fear and anger are about and how they manifest in their life.

Whether you *believe* they are being talked about by others, scrutinized by others, and feeling threatened by others does not matter at the moment, it is this person's very real intralocution, the ongoing and negative beliefs that concern us, and this inner voice is what we are trying to help turn into their conscious awareness.

You now know what your client believes. You want to know the exact words because that is exactly how they speak about themselves in their intralocution. You now hear their self-judgment, the self-condemnation, the belittling they do to themself. You use your client's example of the unknown-other speaking, and you both start working together to clarify who is thinking these words of condescension and what this means regarding their paranoia.

Let us return to our previous dialogue to see how the therapist can use this technique not only to hear the voice of the unknown-other, but to get the client to come to understand whose negative, judgmental thinking this is.

Client: When I walk into that store, everyone stares at me. I don't know any of them, but I know they are judging me and talking about me.

Therapist: You know the people in that store are talking about you. Tell me exactly what they might say about you. Tell me the exact words they would use.

Client: They say, "He's stupid, ugly, weird, look at his hair, his clothes don't even fit him right. Look how fat he is."

Therapist: It sounds like you believe these people are judging you. What else might they be saying about you? Since you believe these people are really judging you, what do they judge in you?

Client: They say things about how shy and lonely I am. They think I'm a pervert. They don't know anything about me. They don't know me, but they judge me anyway.

Therapist: So you go into a store where people see you, but no one really knows you. Now, of everyone in that entire store, maybe a hundred people or so, I have no idea what those people are thinking. Maybe they are thinking about what they are doing there, what's for dinner tonight, or about the argument they just had with their spouse. Anyway, I believe someone is thinking those thoughts about you. In fact, I am convinced, one hundred percent, that someone in that store is thinking those thoughts about you. Someone in that store is saying those negative things about you and judging you. Who do you think is thinking those thoughts and judging you?

Sometimes the client will catch on to what the therapist is asking, sometimes not. The therapist does not know if anyone else in that entire store is thinking the negative thoughts that the client is verbalizing, but they know the client is thinking these thoughts. The real therapeutic dialogue can begin when the client catches on that they are the originator of those thoughts. The client and therapist can now talk about and question beliefs and self-talk regarding negative self-judgments. Appropriate questions such as:

> "How did you start thinking of yourself so negatively, as ugly or weird (or whatever they believe)?"

> "What makes you think you are a pervert?"

> "Tell me about judging yourself so harshly."

> "When did you start putting yourself down as you do?"

Do not lead the client or make suggestions as to what you think is happening to them, or their suspiciousness will rise, or they may think you are trying to read their mind. Listen to their words and ask them how these self-beliefs came to life.

In their quest for privacy, the paranoid person has kept these beliefs, feelings, and self-judgments privately stowed so that others could not get to know them. They would rather keep all this to themself, but by keeping it all so private, these thoughts and beliefs have gained power over them. They may have been so embarrassed by what they believed about them-self that they started suspecting others had these same thoughts about them.

There was possibly a time, in actuality, when others judged them harshly and imposed these names and taunts on them. But with paranoia, the harsh taunts and verbal attacks become self-talk, self-beliefs, and self-judgments. It became their intralocution. They kept quiet out of fear that others would know them and recognize these believed-to-be-true faults about them. The paranoid individual does not want oth-ers to know them for fear that their negative self-beliefs will be exposed, and others will know them for these negative traits.

They do not want others to know them for how they know themself. The fear of being scrutinized and judged by other people is equaled only by the harsh judgment the paranoid individual inflicts upon themself.

Paranoia gives us clues as to the depth of our client's arduous battles of living in his world. Great fear is generated as they talk about how paranoia has attempted to shape the world in which they are now struggling. Knowles writes:

> This understanding of the paranoid character allows the therapist to see that it is the fear that is most basic and so the therapist addresses himself to the client's fear rather than becoming involved in the challenging of the client's perceptions or judgments (Knowles, 1986, p. 45).

Therapy is not an exercise in common sense or logic, and it does no good to use logic and common sense with paranoia. It requires attention to their emotional struggles.

> If the therapist becomes engaged in a rational argument with a specialist in rationality, the therapist will lose and will also stimulate the fear the client already has. ... the therapist should know what he is up against (Knowles, 1986, p. 45).

The paranoid client will protect their fear of talking about their intralocution and confronting their low self-esteem. The therapist must tread lightly here. Be careful of suicidal thoughts when the client is dealing with so much fear. As they work through their many paranoid issues, they may feel unbalanced—too many changes in and around them—and feel that they have nothing familiar to hang on to. What is this fear that has been vaulted? Fear and self-directed anger are the impetus for suicidal thoughts, so, slow is better.

Whatever the outward emotional expression, be it fear or anger, the undisclosed emotion is equally important. For example, if the paranoid client is fearful all the time and expresses their paranoia through fear, we search for the underlying anger that is not or cannot be expressed outwardly. They hold this anger tightly inside so no one can see it and possibly take advantage of them again.

If the paranoid client outwardly expresses themself angrily all the time, we search for the underlying fear which is deeply buried. Fear and anger are equally important while working with paranoia issues. Coming to realize what paranoia is and what it has done to their life is part of this client's individuation process, as will be described in more depth in the next chapter.

Once the client realizes and comes to accept that their intralocution is the voice of the unknown-other, the therapist may give them a homework assignment. The therapist may ask them to go to a crowded place or wherever they usually hear the voice of the unknown-other speaking loudly, and say to themself, "This is me who is speaking; I am saying these things to myself." Slowly, they will realize what they are doing to themself—the voice of the unknown-other has been a substitute for their negative self-esteem and how paranoia has maintained dominance over their life.

ADDRESSING THE COMPLEX

The concept of the complex gives us added depth to work more effectively with paranoia. We know that paranoia acts like a complex, so it had its beginning, its start, somewhere in this person's life, and by using complex theory, we know it had its root when some adult or situation fed incomprehensible doubt, anger, and fear into their life. These early situations were inescapable, emotionally thwarting, and often too overwhelming for the ego. This person's otherwise normal feelings and emotions were repressed, and the complex took root.

By understanding complex theory, we know there is an emotionally charged core within the unconscious of our client that grew into their paranoia. Over the years, this emotional core has grown, possibly unchecked and ineffectively dealt with, and is now a powder keg, ready and willing to explode on anyone who pushes those buttons. We may witness this in therapy.

We know that at the complex's core is an archetypal influence at work. My main focus while describing complex theory was on the mother and father archetypes, identifying the kernel that provided the pathway toward paranoia. Find that influence, and you can then work on those conflicts. Those struggles will be at the core of many of this person's life issues, particularly if their paranoia began at a young age.

As therapy progresses, the therapist may ask the paranoid client, "Did you get along better with one of your parents?" Working with this client's attitudes, problems, feelings, and memories of their parents is no different from what we would do with any client. This may be enough to get them talking about the parent they did not get along with and what had happened to the client. This can become quite emotional. There will be a great deal of anger and fear associated with the memories of those experiences, ranging from dislike to rage to hate. They know they are angry at this parent and need to find the emotional strength to talk about that anger.

I stressed earlier, and I stress it now; we are looking for archetypal influences that were too difficult for this person to handle in their life. We are not necessarily accusing parents of deliberately and consciously violating their charge. When we discover the controlling influence the child could not handle at that time, we can work on that struggle. We are looking for patterns of behavior that our client could not mentally and emotionally cope with, whether it was related to authoritarian control, sexual abuse, domination and control, fear, nervousness, abandonment, being ignored, being emotionally put down and belittled, too much delusion in the home, high expectations and demands that could not be met, being trapped and unable to escape the emotional, physical, or mental abuse and turmoil, among many possible others. As we examine these relationships, we try to understand completely and thoroughly how these early influences were *not* dealt with, what prevented the required emotional expression, and how their life has been changed and disrupted since.

A common question for the therapist would be, "How did these early influences negatively affect this client? What is needed to allow this person to find peace now?" We have to take the time to talk, think, and explore these emotional hardships with our client. It is important to work toward the conscious understanding and integration of these emotionally disturbing issues set in place years before. Jung writes:

> As we know, a complex can be really overcome only if it is lived out to the full. In other words, if we are to develop further we have to draw to us and drink down to the very dregs what, because of our complexes, we have held at a distance (Jung, 1959, pp. 98-99).

In this current world of solution-focused and goal-oriented brief therapies, we will be hard-pressed to do all this integration and to work effectively with paranoia in "ten sessions or less." We need time to work on our client's inherent integration of emotionally distraught memories and paranoid lifestyle. If we have developed trust with them, they may continue working, possibly for years, on integrating their paranoid complex's emotional content, toward the ultimate goal of a stronger personality and individuation.

ADDRESSING SUSPICION

Showing evidence that there is no one out there talking about the paranoid individual does not make them less paranoid. Having others demonstrate proof of the "reality" of things does not change the fact that paranoid individuals are lonely, distrustful, and fearful, and that suspicion and judgmental beliefs dominate their thinking. Trying to prove that they are not paranoid is to doubt what they believe is true for them. Their beliefs may not be factual, logical, or even stand up to common sense, but these are the truths in their life.

Again, any of us can believe anything we want about ourselves or other people. A belief is just a belief, an announcement, a confirmation of what we believe, but there may or may not be any objective truth to what we believe. Telling our client that what they believe and think is not accurate, goes against whom they are as a unique individual and will only support their distrust in you.

The paranoid individual's suspicious beliefs are difficult for them and others to tolerate, inside or outside the therapeutic environment. A faithful wife may feel obligated to show proof to her suspecting husband that she has not broken her marriage vows and is not running around on him, but he will not be convinced. Even if she has evidence of where she was at a certain time, he may say he "forgives" her, but he is not convinced. He will do the same thing to her a few days later.

Suspicion may have nothing to do with the accused, but no one can prove to the suspicious person otherwise. This suspicious thinking is the voice of the unknown-other. The paranoid person hears the unknown-other mocking them, telling them that their spouse is cheating on them, and this only adds to their already existent distrust.

Proof does not make the suspicious person think less about their beliefs; it does not make them brutally judge themself or others any less. Moving far away into the hinterland, miles away from people, will not make the paranoid person believe any less that someone is out there watching them. Installing cameras around their property will not make them believe others are not there and that no one is watching them. Even with video proof that no one is on their property, they will still think and believe that someone is there.

The example from a previous chapter of the woman, while out in her front yard, believed her neighbor, who had recently moved, was staring at her and judging her. Not actually seeing anyone next door, she became convinced that someone must have broken in overnight. Believing that *someone* was over there watching her is an example of not believing the facts. This reminds me of an old saying: "Don't confuse me with the facts; my mind is made up." That would be the response from the paranoid individual when they are presented with evidence that what they are thinking is not based on fact or truth, as a non-paranoid person would realize. Van den Berg states it is an ill-fated attempt to try to show proof to someone who has delusional beliefs.

> He thinks, for instance, that a conspiracy has been set up against him. The healthy person notices nothing of this conspiracy, and he cannot prove to the sick person that he is mistaken. The mentally ill is unaffected by the evidence, no matter how convincing it may be and no matter how much it conforms to reality. ...The mentally ill will not accept the reality of the healthy. His own reality is different. ...The way he relates to the conspiracy is real to him but not to us (van den Berg, 1972, p. 108).

Can we get the suspicious client to accept proof that they are mistaken? I'm not sure we can, but eventually, they may come to realize what is true and what is not, to the best of their ability to do so, through long work in therapy.

WORKING PHASE OF THERAPY

Let me use an example here of someone who has many issues to work through in therapy, layers upon layers of emotional and historical problems. First of all, everyone has a story to tell. One of the first things a client wants to do is tell their story. They talk about what happened to them and the outcome. They focus on who was involved, time, places, reactions, etc. But the therapist wants more. While listening, the therapist hears the depression and says, "Tell me more about your depression."

Now, the client talks about their depression in greater depth. The therapist listens to them talk about their depression, but after a while, the therapist begins to hear the anger in the client's voice, so they say, "Tell me about your anger." Now, the client talks about their anger in great detail with the ongoing encouragement of the therapist. On and on, layer upon layer of emotional struggles is revealed. This is not a rapid process; it could take weeks, months, or even years.

Feelings and experiences range from anxiety, fear, humiliation, disbelief, shame, cognitive dissonance, and abuse. This is the working phase of the client's therapy. I use the following diagram to demonstrate this movement of therapy. Of course, this exact model does not apply to all clients, but this example should suffice to get this idea across.[21]

---

[21] This is only one example, one graphic characterization of what one individual's therapeutic encounter may look like. Any other profile would work here, as long as it eventually leads to the basic root of human psychology, to care about oneself and others.

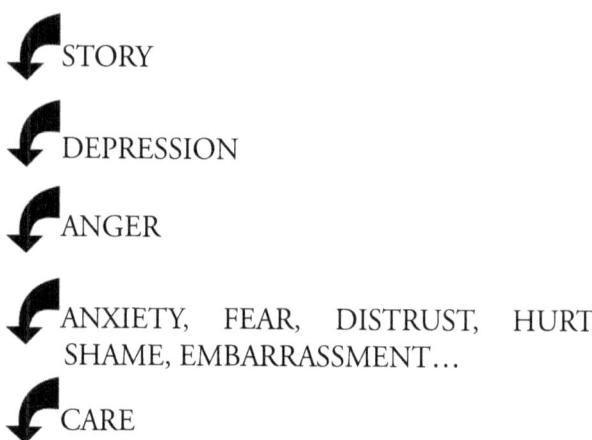

STORY

DEPRESSION

ANGER

ANXIETY, FEAR, DISTRUST, HURT, SHAME, EMBARRASSMENT…

CARE

First, the story must be told. The client needs to describe what they have experienced and the emotional impact it has had on them. While the client is in therapy, they move through a series of progressions and recollections of their depression, anger, anxiety, and so on. As long as the client is moving inward, into their "depth," they are moving along the path toward understanding themself.

We connect on all emotional levels with our clients. The more depth, the more work one must do. But if the client wants to keep returning to the story, they are avoiding responsibility for their depth-work. The therapist only needs to hear a story once, not have it repeated over and over again. The client who constantly returns to their story is slipping off the path of their caring personality, avoiding their true humanity; they are getting sidetracked.

The therapist's job is to bring them back gently, back to the struggle, to the emotions and emotional involvement they have with themself and others—back to *CARE*. Heidegger, in his deep and penetrating analysis of the human being's existence, repeatedly states that *care* is the fundamental and "a priori" condition of existence.

> ...this means it always lies *in* them. ...
> The phenomenon of care in its totality is
> essentially something that cannot be torn
> asunder; so any attempts to trace it back
> to special acts or drives like willing and
> wishing or urge and addiction, or to con-
> struct it out of these, will be unsuccessful
> (Heidegger, 1962, p. 238).

Caring is fundamental to the human being, originally there, but over the years, it can be displaced, ignored, or buried. This does not void care or its importance, for in whatever way people act, behave, or treat others, at the root of being human is "...its state of Being as one whose kind of Being is **care**" (Heidegger, 1962, p. 249).

CARE AND INDIVIDUATION

As we learn more about our paranoid client's thoughts, beliefs, and emotional turmoil, we hear the voice of the unknown-other at work, and we know that voice isn't from without, but it is the usual and degrading intralocution of the paranoid client. They are harsh toward themself. During therapy, we encounter the words of the unknown-other, which tells us how our client is self-degrading and self-judgmental. We learn precisely the words they use against themself. These self-judgmental put-downs are distractions along their path of individuation.

Their antagonistic self-beliefs negatively compromise their personality. Can we help our paranoid client stop these negative self-judgments and learn to care about themself? Can we help them improve their low self-esteem? We can now use their paranoid thoughts, feelings, and judgments to help them bring the negative self-esteem, loneliness, and distrust into consciousness, come to terms with themself, and find a more positive and fulfilling approach to their life. There is nothing unusual about doing this in therapy, whether or not our client is paranoid. But we can now use paranoia as a guide.

SUMMARY

Remember, the word "paranoia" is only a construct that helps us better understand, describe, and identify how this individual's lifestyle controls and torments them. Paranoia is our guide to what lies within, toward this person's current psychological structure that supports this mental illness and disturbance.

Their negative words of ridicule and self-deprecation are not just self-talk for the lone purpose of degrading themself. They are, in fact, patterns of beliefs that have been preventing them from achieving their higher aspirations, their true self-identity. The therapist can help raise the understanding of paranoia from its deep roots in this person's unconscious to a *conscious* level so they can gather hope to settle their suspicions and distrust to healthy levels, to integrate the negativity toward themself into a more livable acceptance of themself, and to assist them on their path through life.

INDIVIDUATION PROCESS

WHY DO WE HAVE TO step outside of most of the major fields of psychology to find references and knowledge of enlightenment, self-actualization, personality integration, and union of spirit and mind? Why does psychology not have more to say about these arcane ideas? Are these only religious bases? Are resolving our emotional problems, learning to deal with stress, confronting and reducing anxiety, behavioral management, and conflict resolution the only goals of therapy with its roots in clinical psychology? What is the push? Where is the focus on the long-term goals of personality integration and individuation, or is psychology and psychotherapy short-sighted?

Some may argue that there are many short-term life conflicts to concern ourselves rather than the total integration of one's personality. Doesn't surviving and getting by in this world, feeling safe, getting a job, having children, raising a family, working, social obligations, and eventual death all trump individuation as long-term processes and goals? How important is it to find out who we truly are as a person, to find out what it means to be...here...now?

The journey toward self-actualization begins by taking all aspects of our lives seriously, dealing with all of our life's struggles, encountering our emotions honestly, using our logic sensitively, improving our relationships, developing our attitudes toward the world, and learning to be our true Self. By self-actualization, we mean the working toward and ongoing attempts to be ourselves, achieving and integrating our purpose, finding our creativity, and striving for our individuality among the hoards of others on this planet.

Individuation is our intended path and ongoing achievement, not necessarily our end goal. We may speak of individuation as a goal, but we will not rest on our laurels after that; this is not the end of the road. We then use our individuation in how we live the rest of our life, individually and among others. Our long-term goals should stretch far enough into the future that death will intercede before we have accomplished all we have intended.

There is no exact recipe for this achievement. It is so personal of an accomplishment that one might say it is between you and your God. Whereas this book is about paranoia, how do we delve into understanding the individuation process, so the paranoid person finds their way through life and their individuality alongside their paranoia? Also, how can we, during therapy, use paranoia to help this person further proceed on their life journey toward individuation? Psychology does have much to offer, but we need to find ways to combine, at least supplement, and complement the various fields of psychology with the long-term individuation process.

The paranoid person feels alone and does not trust people. They think negatively about themself and have tremendous, unresolved fear and anger. They believe others negatively judge them to the point that they seldom want others around. Whom can they talk to about getting better and breaking free of paranoia's control? To be paranoid and talk about it is a great act of courage, risking their current way of living and being in the world as a paranoid person, and it threatens their mental and emotional life as they have lived it for so long. When the paranoid individual risks talking about their paranoia, they risk losing their lonely existence. They are challenged on every level to resolve their life disturbances.

Who will promote the therapeutic goals of a face-to-face encounter with another human needing psychological help and assist those in need of becoming themselves? We must remember that the long-term journey of therapy is the individuation process, and we use that long-term goal—out there toward the future—to spur the paranoid individual toward ultimate integration with themself.

How does one become convinced that a greater understanding and meaning exists in life than only one's day-to-day existence? What kind of life must one live to seek enlightenment, and can the paranoid individual find enlightenment? Pondering deeply over these questions is to initiate one's path toward individuation. No one else can answer these questions for us; we must make the discovery. We must start the search.

Jungian psychology is imbued with the hope and expectation that, ultimately, the individuation process of each person becomes their long-term achievement. Jung defines individuation:

> In general, it is the process by which individual beings are formed and differentiated; in particular, it is the development of the psychological *individual* as a being distinct from the general, collective psychology. Individuation, therefore, is a process of *differentiation,* having for its goal the development of the individual personality (Jung, 1971, p. 448).

Jung uses the word individuation to describe the method of coming to be oneself and consciously realizing it, consciously understanding how one differs from the masses.

ZEN AND INDIVIDUATION

As we find in other philosophies and disciplines, regardless of what word is used to describe this process toward individuation, a great effort is required to pursue an understanding of one's life to the fullest. From Zen, we learn the importance of a single-minded approach toward enlightenment and not allowing anything to come between oneself and eventual enlightenment. Kapleau explains:

> The drive toward enlightenment is powered on the one hand by a painfully felt inner bondage—a frustration with life, a fear of death, or both—and on the other by the conviction that through awakening one can gain liberation. But it is in zazen that the body-mind's force and vigor are enlarged and mobilized for the breakthrough into this new world of freedom. Energies which formerly were squandered in compulsive drives and purposeless actions are preserved and channeled into a unity through correct Zen sitting; and to the degree that the mind attains one-pointedness through zazen it no longer disperses its force in the uncontrolled proliferation of idle thoughts (Kapleau, 1980, pp. 13-14).

According to Zen, our long-term goal of achieving enlightenment should constantly be on our mind, single-mindedly focused, not wavering from it, and totally committed. Through meditation, one learns to slow down one's mind, reduce excessive thinking, and find tranquility. Ongoing meditation feeds this peace for longer periods of time and helps us see the world through more peaceful eyes. Kapleau puts it this way:

Sitting in zazen or meditation has been so accepted as the approved path to spiritual emancipation throughout Asia that no Zen Buddhist had first to be convinced that through it he could develop his powers of concentration, achieve unification and tranquility of mind, and eventually, if his aspiration was pure and strong enough, come to Self-realization (Kapleau, 1980, p. 3).

Zazen is the sitting meditative practice at the heart of one's search for meaning into the nature of one's existence and eventual enlightenment. This meditative practice:

...with the regulation of the breath, the methodical stilling of the thoughts and unification of the mind through special modes of concentration, with the development of control over the emotions and strengthening of the will, and with the cultivation of a profound silence in the deepest recesses of the mind—in other words, through the practice of zazen—there are established the optimum preconditions for looking into the heart-mind and discovering there the true nature of existence (Kapleau, 1980, p. 9).

Now Zen is a different animal than psychology, but both work toward a similar goal, that of finding oneself, one's individual nature. Working with a Zen master can be a path out of paranoia.

The enlightenment for which Zen aims, for which Zen exists, comes of itself. As consciousness, one moment it does not exist,

the next it does. But physical man walks
in the element of time even as he walks in
mud, dragging his feet and his true nature
(Reps, 1961, p. 133).

The Zen story of the ten bulls is an ancient demonstration
of not only the initiation of the enlightenment process, but the
ongoing living-out of the individuated person.[22]

The bull is the eternal principle of life,
truth in action. The ten bulls represent
sequent steps in the realization of one's true
nature (Reps, 1961, p. 134).

When one reads and studies this story, one finds a connection to one's process of discovery and how one's paranoia can
be the catalyst for one's individuation process. One discovers
where to begin as one turns from the voice of the unknown-
other to focus on one's intralocution.

CHRISTIAN PERSPECTIVE ON INDIVIDUATION

From a Christian perspective, 16th-century Christian mystic
John of the Cross says one must struggle to achieve "union with
God," the theological and spiritual parallel of psychology's individuation process. Speaking of the spiritual union of the human
soul while on earth, John of the Cross says:

The attainment of our goal demands that
we never stop on this road, which means
we must continually get rid of our wants
rather than indulging them. For if we do

---

[22] Read, for example, Paul Reps, *Zen Flesh, Zen Bones*, which includes
the story of "The Ten Bulls," Anchor Books, NY.

not get rid of them all completely, we will not wholly reach our goal. The log of wood cannot be transformed into the fire that even a single degree of heat is lacking to its preparation for this. The soul, similarly, will not be transformed into God even if it has only one imperfection. As we shall explain in speaking of the night of faith, a person has only one will and if that is encumbered or occupied by anything, the person will not possess the freedom, solitude, and purity requisite for divine transformation (Saint John, 1991, p. 144).

I will not confuse psychology and theology, for psychology speaks of thoughts, feelings, emotions, relationships, and how we may help others and transform ourselves toward good mental health while we are still on earth. Theology and western religions try to help us address our existence and our relationship with God, but they teach that we have few options but to delay the union of our spiritual life with God until after death, after our individual psychology has come to an end. Why does religion instruct us to "delay" our human need for individuation until after death?

Psychology differs from the theological view in that we humans can never expect to achieve perfection and should never live our life based on being "perfect." Humans are not perfect and can never expect to be perfect, so we do not equate individuation to mean the same as perfection. It is not. Good mental health is not guaranteed; it may be our future, but we must work toward it. The struggle toward mental health becomes the individuation process.

ANXIETY AND THE INDIVIDUATION PROCESS

One of the earliest and most powerful challenges in our personal psychology is our confrontation with anxiety. How can we achieve any sort of individuation when we must contend with anxiety and its control over our life? Anxiety can *stimulate* the individuation process. It is an *a priori* condition of paranoia, and we must encounter and deal with our ongoing anxiety, not only alongside paranoia, but also alongside our entire developmental and individuation process.

What is this power we call anxiety? What control does it have over life, and what is its purpose? Anxiety is the first, the last, and the greatest psychological threat one must encounter before one dies. Does our inescapable death force us to face anxiety and learn from it, or do we turn and run from it? Tillich would have us think about this:

> Fate would not produce inescapable anxiety without death behind it. And death stands behind fate and its contingencies not only in the last moment when one is thrown out of existence but in every moment within existence. Nonbeing is omnipresent and produces anxiety even where an immediate threat of death is absent. It stands behind the experience that we are driven, together with everything else, from the past toward the future without a moment of time which does not vanish immediately. It stands behind the insecurity and homelessness of our social and individual existence. It stands behind the attacks on our power of being in body and soul by weakness, disease, and accident. In all these forms fate actualizes itself, and through them the anx-

iety of nonbeing takes hold of us (Tillich, 1952/2000, p. 45).

Tillich writes that "nonbeing" is our ultimate profound psychological threat. This is death anxiety, the fact that life has a beginning and an end, and activates the question of whether or not there is any real purpose or meaning to life. One establishes meaning and purpose through living, but is there an ultimate purpose for *our* life?

Anxiety is exacerbated when one:

- becomes aware of oneself.
- is sharing time and space with others.
- realizes one's ultimate finitude and the fate of non-being.
- realizes one may be living a life without purpose or meaning.

Does our encounter with anxiety *propel* us toward individuation or *prevent* us from walking our path toward psychological fulfillment? Anxiety is a double-edged sword. It impels us to run in fear, from ourselves and the world, and it slices through the idiosyncrasies and dross of life to help us discover what is important to our unique existence. How we treat our anxiety is a decision we must each make consciously: for fulfillment, nothingness, or suffering.

SETTING GOALS

Throughout life, it would benefit us to ask ourselves consciously, what are my long-term goals? Have I established long-term psychological goals yet? What is it that I want out of my life? What do I want to achieve: mentally, physically, psychologically, emotionally, spiritually, and socially? If I take the time to think about my long-term goals, this puts me on a path toward achieving those goals.

As an illustration, let us say I am traveling and want my ultimate destination to be New York City.[23] Since I currently do not live close to New York City, getting there would be a distant goal for me, especially since I would have to walk alone. There is no external GPS guiding our life, and we all must walk through our life basically alone; no one can carry any of us to the end.

So, I set off for New York City, and all decisions I make will hopefully point me toward my destination so I may eventually get there. That sounds very simple. But without foreknowledge and planning, I may set off on a journey without actually considering my goal and may have no idea where I want to go. I just wander, always taking one well-worn side road after another or possibly a road less traveled. I may get lost. I may meet others along the way who do not share my destination and, feeling defeated, live my life among them. I may never get to my ultimate intended goal, and I soon forget that I even had a destination in the first place. I forget that I have an intended life journey.

This happens to the person who has made their long-term goal something short of complete individuation. They get sidetracked and lose their way, ending up always feeling short of fulfillment, as if something is always missing.

So let us say I eventually accomplish what I set out to do, and I reach New York City. What do I do now? I have reached a goal that was always there but inaccessible until I set out on my journey to succeed in this life task. I cannot just sit in a park and feed birds, meditate, or daydream all day; I must now continue to integrate all of what this city and the world have to offer and

---

[23] If you live in or near New York City, you might change this example destination to a far-away city such as Los Angeles, California. If you live in a country other than the United States, pick a city that is a great distance from you.

all the possibilities that I have to offer this city and the world. But what does this mean?

What if I do not consciously know there is a psychological/spiritual direction that I can travel that eventually leads to a place where I can call home and feel eased of the burdens of a long struggle? Individuation is that kind of journey. Once I have achieved some measure of individuation and at least know who I am and why I am making my decisions the way I do, what will I now do with myself? Approaching this goal allows one clear insight into why one set out on this journey in the first place.

Individuation is our long-term goal, but it is not the end of our journey. The journey is our life. It takes a great deal of courage and resolve to follow a path that one does not initially fully understand, a path that is felt in one's marrow, that one only slowly becomes consciously aware of as one trudges along through life. At some point, one must consciously resolve to follow one's path. One may meander at first, but one needs to be resolute, connect to oneself, and be oneself.

One can now direct conscious attention to one's psychological and spiritual needs and ultimate hope of accomplishing mental and emotional health. One steps out of the common ground of everydayness, away from the hordes, away from the collective.

> Nobody can give directions for the actions of the "resolute" individual—no God, no conventions, no laws of reason, no norms or principles. *We* must be ourselves, *we* must decide where to go. Our conscience is the call to ourselves. It does not tell anything concrete, it is neither the voice of God nor the awareness of eternal principles. It calls us to ourselves out of the behavior of the average man, out of daily talk, the daily routine... (Tillich, 1952/2000, p. 148).

PARANOIA AND INDIVIDUATION

Paranoia is a way of living, suffering in life through suspicion, distrust, and loneliness, but it also helps us identify the roots of our suffering. Understanding paranoia helps the paranoid individual identify what they need to do to get started moving along their path of individuation.

The paranoid individual does not initially believe the truth; they are suspicious of it. They may only know the menial and mundane, the loneliness and distrust, and the minimization of one's achievements. Without knowing what kind of life is possible, how can the paranoid individual's long-term life goal be anything but short of individuation? I would venture to say that most paranoid people do not even realize they can live a psychologically happy and fulfilled life. If one's life experience is paranoid, one's journey toward individuation will then be experienced through paranoia.

Paranoia prevents one from knowing that there is more to life than distrust and the daily self-condemnation and suspiciousness. If we do not know where we are, what we are capable of, and where we want to be someday, how will we ever get there?

The paranoid person's proclivity to life is like the blinds on one's windows. The blinds keep the paranoid person closed off, hidden in the darkness of their loneliness and individual thoughts. They want no one looking in on them. One paranoid client stated, "I keep my blinds drawn tight so that others cannot see me, and I don't have to see them. I can remain hidden."

They fear being seen, observed, and discovered. They feel protected behind the blinds, but not really. They are interested in the outside world. They peek out from behind the blinds to see who is there, who is looking in on them, who is interested in them, and who is making those disparaging remarks. They are curious, their eyes darting back and forth, looking, searching for the unknown-other. They may believe the blinds protect them, but their anxiety makes them peer outside with constant vigilance. They have a choice; stay hidden, look beyond the blinds using their physical eye, or use their psychological "eye" to seek the truth about the unknown-other.

They may use their psychological eye to find their way inward toward their as-of-yet-unrealized self-judgment and self-scrutiny that has minimized their acceptance and importance of themself. This psychological eye is watchful, penetrating, and revealing. Edinger (1995) believed that the "eye of God" is the archetype being activated with paranoia. He believed one's ego "projects" the eye of God onto the world, so "the ego has the experience of being watched, listened to, persecuted" (p. 67) by others.

This eye looks both ways, although initially internally muddled, until one realizes that the voice of the unknown-other is one's own intralocution, and what one fears the most is the direction one needs to go. The dual nature of the blind is a metaphor for the paranoid life; it keeps one hidden from the outside world, and also hidden from oneself. It encourages one to search "out there" for help and prevents one from finding one's true self internally.

Using the personal pronoun, if I turn my eyes toward my own life, put my attention on what the unknown-other's voice is telling me about myself, I am directing my thoughts and energies toward the possibility of moving along my individuation path. By acknowledging the voice of the unknown-other as my intralocution, I can now find my way back to myself, away from the undeveloped, unrealized, and unacknowledged sides of my paranoid personality.

The "I" or inner "eye" that saw itself for the first time in infancy during the mirror phase at the birth of the ego can now see itself again as the "I" working on one's individuation process. When the ego is born, the individuation process begins and continues throughout life if it doesn't get waylaid, blocked, or forgotten. One's ego continues to evolve and develop through one's education, growth, maturity, and developmental experiences. Does one have the foresight of this long-term goal, or does one bumble along the way until one forgets one even has the *need* to achieve self-understanding and enlightenment?

A Conscious Beginning

A thirty-something young man came to therapy seeking help for depression. After a clearing process, he identified pent-up anger towards his father as much of the reason he felt so depressed. He stated that his father had attempted suicide several years before, and he, the son, was blamed by the father for "causing" him to attempt suicide. The son believed this and felt obligated to make his father's life better. The son now was at the father's beck and call, blindly and unconsciously accepting the "servant" label, and gave up his life to "save" his father, to walk in his father's responsibility instead of his own. A couple of years later, the father attempted another suicide and again blamed the son. The longer the younger man talked about this in therapy, the angrier he became. His psychological eye was opening.

One day, out of great anger, he forcefully stated, "I am not my father's keeper," and he would no longer accept blame for his father's actions. At that moment, the son began consciously attending to his individuation. He could no longer accept his position as slave or savior. He was now willing to walk his own life and decide his own decisions. The reason I feel this story is significant is that the son had finally accepted his own life and was now willing to make his own conscious direction, his need for self-actualization taking over. He could no longer live blindly; he now saw the truth of his decisions and actions. This contributed to his conscious individuation process.

UNDERSTANDING THE INDIVIDUATION PROCESS

For a moment, I would like to equate the individuation process to the sport of American football. If I want to know what it is like to play football, I will not learn by sitting on the bench and watching others play. I need to get in there and experience it with my body. I need to learn the rules, feel the hits, and feel myself inside my helmet. I would certainly benefit from having a good, knowledgeable coach, but *I* must play the game.

The vast majority of people sit on the proverbial "life bench," not really playing the game, not really participating fully in life. They eventually get bored, sit and watch TV, hang out on their cell phone all day, throw themselves into their work, do drugs or alcohol, or play video games, spending the rest of their life wasting away. If I want to know something about myself, I cannot just sit on the sidelines and allow too much anxiety, boredom, or laziness to take over my life. I begin first by knowing there is a "Self" and being interested in my "Self." Then, I need to learn, investigate, search for answers, and ponder my life. I must live my life to the fullest by getting out and physically living. I would also benefit from having a "coach."

Using a different metaphor, let me speak about the study of biology. If I want to understand biology, I will need to find an excellent book, take some classes, and find a worthwhile teacher who knows and understands biology. Then, I need to learn and study biology, reflect on my new knowledge and absorb it. The teacher must know biology well enough so they can explain it. Actual life practice and structured lab work help with hands-on learning.

But, unlike the tomes of biology already written, there is no book on my shelf with my name on it that will explain to me just what I must do to learn about myself and work my individuation path. I (Self) must be the book I wish was on my shelf, and I need to start reading about "me" through self-examination.

Using our imagination for a moment, let us say you were one of the luckiest persons alive, one of the 8 billion humans currently living on earth, and you found a book with your name on the cover, and it contained everything about your life, everything you need to know to make you finally realize who you are and for what purpose you serve on earth. The title of this book would be "<u>Your Name</u>."

So that you will remember the date you found this book, write today's date here _____.[24]

Now, open this book and start reading. What does your book say about you and your life's lessons? Who are you, and who are you supposed to be? Does your book contain more facts about you, or have some chapters yet to be written? Can you find your memories? Does it include your nighttime dreams and messages from your unconscious? Where is the chapter on how you became paranoid?

What you have found here is a book of mirrors, each page another reflection of you and your life. Each page makes you look at yourself and reflect upon yourself throughout your greatly nuanced life. But, recalling the chapter on loneliness, we are not islands to ourselves. We need others to assist us out of our loneliness and into insight. We need others to show us when we are off course. Too many mirrors can make us narcissistic or self-degrading.

As with many learning experiences, we benefit from having a teacher point us in the right direction when we get lost. Where do we go to find a worthy and knowledgeable teacher? Who can you begin talking to about your life? If seeking therapy, you would benefit from finding a therapist who has been

---

[24] Go ahead and write today's date on the line above. Use ink. Someday, if you happen to reread this book or are looking up something about paranoia, you will discover how much time has passed since you attempted this effort of self-discovery; possibly in pursuit of your individuation goals or realizing how much time has passed not in that pursuit.

traveling their individual path for much of their years. There is an old saying, "When the student is ready, the teacher will appear."

Never accept a therapist who has not been in analysis first. Having an unskilled or inexperienced teacher only produces more shadows. There is a long road ahead. Paranoid people have many unfulfilled needs. It may prevent them from recognizing and fulfilling their needs. But if, as the Buddha says, all humans are capable of enlightenment, then it makes no sense to say that a paranoid individual could not work toward that goal. Religious in-depth studies teach us how to reflect on the deadly sins of life and eventually find our ultimate spiritual conversion. However, like most human struggles for advancement, one cannot do it all alone. We all need some help over the hurdles.

Neumann describes the result of this long, tedious work toward individuation as:

> ...an expression of the fact that a total constellation of the personality has been reached, in which the creativeness of the psyche and the positiveness of the conscious mind no longer function like two opposed systems split off from one another, but have achieved a synthesis (Neumann, 1954, p. 414).

Being conscious and acting intentionally is not a great effort; it is quite natural, although getting to a completely conscious state may take years to achieve. If one continues to find it difficult to be conscious of certain aspects of life, then those life situations still need attention because they continue to produce conflict, confusion, and control over our conscious mind. Too many thoughts can lead to too many emotions and confusion, adding to the struggles of living a conscious life.

MASLOW'S PYRAMID

Understanding Maslow's pyramid gives the paranoid individual his direction in life as they attempt to move along their path to self-actualization. Maslow identifies various needs of the human being and states that each level of need must be met before the next level can be fully attained (see fig. A). The lines separating the levels within the pyramid graphic appear to be rigid, but they are not actual boundaries; each level flows one into the other. As we consciously focus on our various needs, really work on our struggles with this or that aspect of our life, all levels will be affected in some way. The paranoid person struggles on most or all levels.

If the paranoid individual is homeless, this can be particularly troublesome because of their distrust of others. Their suspiciousness may be so great that they try to survive without the basic needs of life. Whether living in a homeless shelter or on the streets, they may not have enough food or water to survive and may stay isolated because of their distrust. The voice of the unknown-other speaks loudly, and without others to talk to them daily, they are absorbed in listening to the unknown-other.

Fig. (A) Maslow's Pyramid

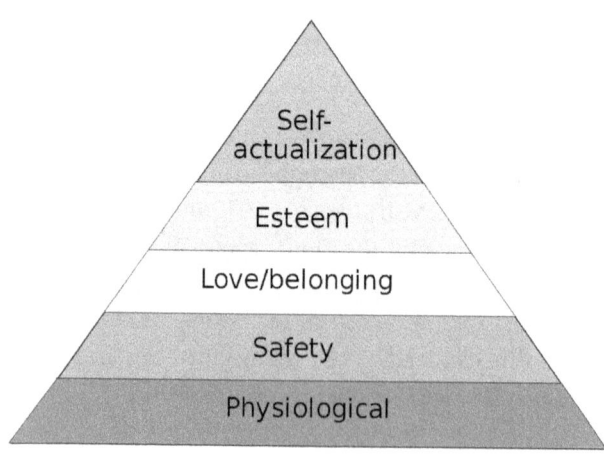

If the paranoid individual has their basic survival needs met, Maslow states that they must then contend with physical and psychological safety needs. They do not feel safe; they are suspicious and distrustful of others. They hear the voice of the unknown-other and believe it is coming from people who are "out there." They believe they are judged negatively and will be harmed. They avoid others who are trying to help them.

If the paranoid person feels some sense of safety in the world, their belief that others are out to get them reduces. They connect with their need to belong, attempt to feel comfortable among others, and believe others can care about them. They are usually not comfortable around people and would prefer to spend more time alone; love and belonging are kept at a distance. If they do not want to take on the responsibility of being a friend, they will continue to struggle with loneliness vs. companionship. They benefit from facing their paranoia, dealing with loneliness and trust issues, and the innate desire to belong to and among others.

Maslow's next identified need is one's ability to have positive self-esteem and to feel as if they are worthy. They want to feel capable and believe they can find self-worth. Maslow describes how important self-esteem is to well-being:

> All people in our society (with a few pathological exceptions) have a need or desire for a stable, firmly based, (usually) high evaluation of themselves, for self-respect, or self-esteem, and for the esteem of others. By firmly based self-esteem, we mean that which is soundly based upon real capacity, achievement and respect from others. ... Satisfaction of the self-esteem need leads to feelings of self-confidence, worth, strength, capability and adequacy of being useful and

> necessary in the world. But thwarting of
> these needs produces feelings of inferiority,
> of weakness and of helplessness (Maslow,
> 1943/2013, p. 7).

Poor self-esteem is central to paranoia, and as the paranoid individual progresses through the hierarchy of needs, they slowly grapple with negative self-esteem. It is with their self-esteem that understanding the voice of the unknown-other points to how they think and feel about themself, and their identity. Since they have listened to and believed the voice of the unknown-other, they now challenge their negative self-evaluation. They face themself and their negativity, slowly shifting from self-doubt to self-efficacy and accomplishment.

The paranoid individual benefits from tapping into their creativity, achieving a higher purpose for themself, and believing that they are a good, worthwhile person whom others can and do like. As the paranoid individual works on self-esteem issues, their ability to subdue the negative voice of the unknown-other increases.

> The tragedy of many people's lives is that
> they look for self-esteem in every direc-
> tion except within, and so they fail in their
> search. In this book we shall see that posi-
> tive self-esteem is best understood as a spir-
> itual attainment, that is, *as a victory in the
> evolution of consciousness* (Branden, 1994,
> pp. 52-53).

Maslow does not stop with self-esteem. He believes humans are capable of achieving more; an ongoing striving for morality, creativity, problem-solving acumen, acceptance and tolerance for all people, and one's ability to care about oneself and others, i.e., self-actualization.

> Self-actualization has particular signifi-
> cance for Abraham Maslow, who holds
> that one has within oneself proclivity
> toward growth and unity of personality
> and a type of inherent blueprint or pattern
> consisting of a unique set of characteristics
> and an automatic thrust toward expressing
> them. ...As these needs are met, then the
> individual turns toward satisfying self-ac-
> tualizing needs which consist of cognitive
> needs—knowledge, insight, wisdom—and
> esthetic needs—symmetry, congruence,
> integration, beauty, meditation, creativity,
> harmony (Yalom, 1980, p. 438).

Through the lifespan, one's overreaching need is to work toward self-actualization. It may not be something one is always consciously working on, but it is an actual human *need* to become self-actualized. As one struggles with one's needs, one develops a stronger and stronger *ethic* to continue working toward self-fulfillment and self-actualization.

> All nature seeks this goal and finds it ful-
> filled in man, but only in the most highly
> developed and most fully conscious man.
> Every advance, even the smallest, along
> the path of conscious realization adds that
> much to the world (Jung, 1959, p. 96).

The need of the human spirit is to be self-actualized and fulfilled. If one is not striving and working toward self-actual-ization, one feels a deep sense of guilt for wasting one's life and not achieving all of what one could be. This is existential guilt, the actual guilt of wasting one's life, of not achieving or work-ing toward whom one is capable of being in one's greatest and most personal way. The further one moves away from whom one is—in all of one's talents, creativeness, and moral inter- and intra- personal ways—one experiences guilt. May describes the importance of understanding the difference between existential guilt and other forms of guilt.

> Let us note well that…the patient *is* guilty, not merely that he *has guilt feelings.* This is a radical statement with far-reaching implications. It is an existential approach which cuts through the dense fog which has obscured much of the psychological discussion of guilt—discussions that have proceeded on the assumption that we can deal only with some vague "guilt feelings," as though it did not matter whether guilt was real or not (May, 1983, p. 114).

This is real guilt, the guilt of not achieving because of ignorance, laziness, grief, self-doubt, paranoia, greed, or any choice one has made to avoid one's responsibility to one's Self and one's life. If one is not working toward psychological and spiritual health, then one is guilty.

Becoming self-fulfilled can take years of therapeutic work—with a teacher, therapist, master, guru, mentor, sensei, spiritual confessor—but this is the necessary work required to achieve individuation and surpass paranoia. Paranoia must be confronted consistently, and only then can an increasing ability to trust and improved self-esteem be slowly integrated into one's conscious personality. No one makes the conscious determination that one day they are self-actualized. The individual who has worked toward individuation over long years comes to realize:

> After passing through all the phases of world-experience and self-experience, the

individual reaches consciousness of his true meaning. He knows himself the beginning, middle, and end of the self-development of the psyche, which manifests itself first as the ego and is then experienced by this ego as the self (Neumann, 1954, p. 416).

THE BENEFIT OF OPPOSITES

Through much of our psychological development, we are confronted with opposite ideas, situations, relationships, and emotions that automatically conflict with each other. This is a conscious/unconscious phenomenon. Our conscious understanding of the world tends to be "this way" and not "that way." When we are in a situation or event that exposes us to a different way, often quite the opposite, our mind becomes confused, surprised, guarded, and challenged. Actually, we need these psychological struggles to achieve anything worthwhile in life. When we are met with a difficult situation or problem, the unconscious mind becomes activated, exposing the positive and negative aspects of the situation, and we must now consciously resolve this conflict.

The opposites will also identify what we like and dislike, the sad and happy, the peaceful and chaotic, the left side of an argument, and the right side of that same argument.[25] Opposites are very important. Often we do not recognize or see the opposite, focusing rather on only one aspect of the conflict, either the "this way" or the "that way," but the opposite is always there somewhere; we may have to look for it and then work to resolve the differences.

---

[25] The opposites show themselves through contrast: night/day, good/evil, bendable/constricted, pain/pleasure, up/down, sad/happy, male/female, loneliness/companionship, etc. Once a conflict arises, the opposite set the parameters for resolution and integration.

> The self-differentiating structure of the psyche is reflected in a world cleft asunder by the principle of opposites into outside and inside, conscious and unconscious, life and spirit, male and female, individual and collective. …For humanity as a whole and the single individual have the same task, namely, to realize themselves as a unity (Neumann, 1954, p. 417).

Sometimes one may seek the opposite just for the fun of the challenge, needling the conflict to decrease and broaden one's narrow understanding. Opposites are like the swinging pendulum on an old grandfather clock. They cannot stay naturally suspended to the left peak or the right peak for long; they will always seek balance somewhere in between.

Ian's Struggle

Ian is a lonely teenager who craves friendships. He is torn between his current lonely life and his imagination and hope of someday having a friend. He thinks of himself as a humanitarian, but he currently sees no way of actively living as such. This contrast between loneliness and friendship, the opposites in his thinking, emotions, and life-struggle, confirms the reality he experiences, and it tears him apart. This contradiction cannot currently be resolved. He is being driven psychologically to find a solution. How will his mind solve this impasse?

If Ian holds this tension of opposites within him, allowing it to burn within and consume him, and if he talks about it in therapy, there is a great possibility that he will resolve his conflict, move toward less isolation, and slowly toward what he can only imagine for himself: having a friend. This tension of opposites pushes Ian a little further along his path of individuation toward his life, where personal interactions are sought on many levels. He is teetering between opposites, which may continue for many years. Hopefully, and eventually, he may find his solutions and fulfillment through resolving the opposites.

SUMMARY

By shifting their attention from the voice of the unknown-other to their intralocution, the paranoid person identifies: what concerns them the most; their innermost snide beliefs about themselves; what is most undesirable about them to themselves; and the negative self-evaluation from which they wish to be freed. Paranoia exposes—making this self-estrangement known—how they hold themself back from understanding themself consciously.

The eventual integration, the working through the often unadmitted negative self-evaluation and self-condemnation, eventually leads to a better understanding of themself and moves them along their unique life-path.

As discussed in the previous chapter, Heidegger states that to *be* a human being is to *care*. Once we can attend to our ability to care, if initially only about ourselves, we walk the path of enlightenment. If care gets blurred over the years under piles of anger, distrust, anxiety, paranoia, narcissism, depression, embarrassment, shame, and being told one is no good and won't amount to much, belittled, taken advantage of, or abused, one's ability to care can get buried.

With great effort and time, one can slowly return with confidence to one's ability to "care." Ultimately, the self-actualized individual is the person who has returned to "care," to the ability to care about themself and their fellow human beings. Very important to restate: The self-actualized individual is the person who has returned to "care," to their ability to care genuinely about themself and their fellow human beings.

FINAL THOUGHTS

E ACH CHAPTER IN THIS BOOK is about a different topic, but combined, they form an understanding of paranoia meant to be read as a whole. Just like life, we do not live with isolated thoughts, feelings, beliefs, or actions. We live our life as a complete individual, with flaws and all. As intelligent beings, we can separate various thoughts, goals, and ideas for further investigation and analysis, as I have done here chapter by chapter, but we cannot sustain this separateness and effectively live our life with meaningfulness. It is this way with paranoia as well. We must understand paranoia through its constituents, but also in its entirety, just as we work with and accept our paranoid clients in their entirety while we investigate various aspects of their lives that include paranoia.

Upon separating paranoia into its finer constituents for investigative purposes, I now need to throw them back together, reintegrate the dissection, and talk about paranoia as it is lived, as a mild annoyance in some people, or as a serious mental disorder of varying degrees by others. The longer paranoia lives and affects one's life, the more integrated it becomes into one's personality. An occasional suspiciousness does not make one's entire life paranoid. However, the longer one lives in fear, suspicion, loneliness, low self-esteem, and distrust without ongoing intervention with healthy others, the more paranoia becomes a disorder of the personality, affecting one's entire life, through and through, in thoughts, feelings, beliefs, relationships, and actions.

LEARNING FROM PETER

It wasn't until Peter came into therapy—whom we first met in the Introduction and throughout—that I started seeing paranoia as an under-examined psychological phenomenon whose depth needed to be plumbed and understood. Helpful literature was scant, so writing this book became my engagement in the mystery of the paranoia phenomenon. I invited others—students, clients, and volunteers—who believed they were paranoid, to write descriptions of themselves when they were paranoid—what they believed, how they felt, and how they handled all this in their daily life. Through these written descriptions of paranoia, common underlying themes emerged.

This process turned out to be "a mountain to be climbed and not a flower to be plucked" (Zen quote) for the next many years. I searched for answers. Why do paranoid individuals believe they are the center of everyone's attention? Why do they believe others find them so fascinating that they are talked about every time they are in public? Why do they retreat toward isolation? Individuals who are paranoid are not only paranoid in their thoughts and beliefs, but they are also paranoid, suspicious, distrusting, lonely, and have low self-esteem throughout everyday life. They try to hide, so others do not notice their negative traits, but these lonely individuals continue to believe everyone is against them and do not realize that they are indeed their own worst enemy.

My Research Findings

One can be paranoid without consciously being aware of it. They may suspect something is wrong, and others may tell them something is just not right with them, but their paranoid thoughts tell them it's *others* who have a problem.

One of the most important outcomes of this research is the understanding of the *voice of the unknown-other*. If you talk with a paranoid person, they will tell you they can actually *hear* the voice of the unknown-other, but what they believe they hear is not with their ears. They believe others "out there" are talking about them, and they vindicate themself with their beliefs. This is their attempt to prevent themself from consciously realizing and acknowledging the otherwise unacceptable beliefs they have of themself.

We now know the voice of the unknown-other is their own intralocution, the inner conversation used to understand and make sense of their world. The voice of the unknown-other is the worst of their self-condemnation and low self-esteem being brought to the fore. It is their way of hiding and protecting themself from *themself*. This voice tells of the deep fears that need to be examined. They must develop trust, preferably with a skilled and knowledgeable therapist, so that they can challenge themself and work around their fears, get to the negative core of self-deprecating beliefs that now dominate their conscious and unconscious mind.

As they truly look at themself and their paranoia, there is a greater possibility of integrating into consciousness the discordance that the voice of the unknown-other identifies. This does not mean a complete extrication of paranoia, but a greater possibility of settling down the fear, anger, loneliness, and distrust, and improving authentic self-esteem.

Paranoia is the distrust we have built up toward others. It tells us that the eyes of the unknown-other are always upon us, and erroneously, that the persecutor is out there. To better understand our own paranoia, we must listen consciously to our thoughts, to the actual words we use in our intralocution that describe us to ourselves.

PARANOIA AS PROACTIVE

What are the words we hear from the unknown-other? We initially do not recognize this as our thinking, but it is us; it is not a "demon" or anyone else talking about us. We are our own critics who judge ourselves. What derogatory put-downs do you use against yourself? Will you say those words out loud so that your ears, and others, will hear you? We need to speak openly about the voice of the unknown-other with a trusted person, get it out of intralocution solely and into interlocution, to an actual conversation with others. With the recognition of the voice of the unknown-other as our own intralocution, we can turn our paranoia from *reactive* to now taking a *proactive* approach. We can now address our inner negative beliefs and low self-esteem and do something about them.

With this recognition, we will not need to look outside to find the negative condemnation. The studied and examined voice of the unknown-other moves us inward, toward our self-healing, toward finding out what is so disturbing in our psyche that prevents us from living peacefully. No longer does the voice of the unknown-other control or tell us what we think and do. We can consciously become our own judge for the betterment. We now have the opportunity to inspect, analyze, and do the necessary work to raise our low pseudo self-esteem, move toward a more holistic understanding of our paranoia, and turn it into something productive and worthwhile, i.e., pursuing our individual life-path.

As we correct the negative attitudes and beliefs we have about ourselves, we grow in authentic self-esteem. If we pay attention to our inner conversation, our intralocution, we no longer project our thoughts onto others, but engage in self-healing, self-understanding. We integrate into our conscious personality all that we learn about ourselves. We increase our chances of being less lonely. With open communication, including communion with trustworthy people, we lower the appeal for isolation and possibly learn to trust someone.

The voice of the unknown-other has been telling us what we are afraid to recognize about ourselves. That voice tells us what we fear others will discover about our negativity. Paranoia has us live fearfully, believing that others will discover who we are and what we hide about ourselves, even if what we believe is not and never was true. We can now confront our delusions. Paranoia remains a difficult hindrance to living consciously until we recognize it for what it is. When we attend to our paranoia and become consciously aware of ourselves, we better understand where the actual threats come from, not from outside, but from within ourselves.

> Awareness is his knowing that something is threatening from outside in his world—a condition which may, as in paranoids and their neurotic equivalents, be correlated with a good deal of acting-out behavior. But self-consciousness puts this awareness on a quite different level; it is the patient's seeing that *he is the one who is threatened*, that he is the being who stands in this world which threatens, he is the subject who *has* a world. And this gives him the possibility of *in-sight*, of "inward sight," of seeing the world and its problems in relation to himself. And thus it gives him the possibility of doing something about the problems (May, 1983, p. 31).

Getting to the Roots of Paranoia

It is possible that the roots of paranoia began in childhood. As one of the key components undergirding the phenomenon of paranoia, loneliness confronts the child who spends too much time alone and has limited familial and social interactions. Children who do not talk about their thoughts or feelings could be more at risk. Those who are told to keep quiet, are often punished, feel unloved and not cared for, or experience abuse may be prone to developing paranoia.

After about the age of five or six, when children's audible self-talk becomes private speech, adults can no longer hear what children are thinking. Except for adults who keep up with the inner dialogue of children through communication and listening, and by being receptive to children's feelings, most others lose the opportunity to know what children are thinking and how they view their world.

As has been spelled out, having close friends is particularly important in middle and pre-adolescent childhood, as it not only prepares them for many of the trials of adolescence, but also helps to moderate some of their distorted and incorrect thinking, chiefly about themselves. By encouraging complete and open dialogue through meaningful communication, we, as trusting and caring adults, can keep an open, trusting, and friendly dialogue with children as they grow toward adolescence. Children may then be more likely to talk about their beliefs and feelings with us well into adolescence, when loneliness and low self-esteem are possibly a substantial risk. The real importance for the child is to have a mature, mentally well-adjusted adult to talk to about problems and life questions.

PERSONAL UNCONSCIOUS MIND

What we psychologically hide from ourselves is sometimes only a question and answer away: "What don't I know about myself?" What we have forgotten about ourselves is subjugated to the personal unconscious mind, but it remains influential. The personal unconscious:

> It includes all those psychic contents which have been forgotten during the course of the individual's life. Traces of them are still preserved in the unconscious, even if all conscious memory of them has been lost (Jung, 1960/1969, p. 310).

The personal unconscious holds many of the answers to what we believe are "unknown" to us. The conscious mind has an awe-inspiring ability to figure out problems with careful and proper challenges, questions, and attention put to those problems.

For example, when we work on trust issues, all conscious and unconscious materials related to trust will be affected. While addressing loneliness, all aspects of loneliness, both conscious and unconscious, shift around a little. The imaginary division that separates our conscious mind from our unconscious mind, what I have called the "I don't know" line, begs us to go just a little further and answer one more question regarding what we don't know. So "I don't know" can often be a valid, correct answer to many of our life's questions, but this answer is unfulfilling.

Understanding oneself, who one truly is in one's Being, is not impossible to realize, but it is hidden. We are obligated, out of necessity, to search out our answers, either alone or by finding someone we trust and with whom we can open up about our thoughts, beliefs, fears, anger, distrust, loneliness, negative self-image, and relationship struggles. We are autonomous beings regarding what we know, think, and believe, and it is up to each of us to figure that out.

REESTABLISHING CARE

With diligent attention to the underlying constituents, paranoia may become less of the "exclusive" life focus, but one focus among all of our other psychological conflicts. Over time, one may eventually become more consciously aware of one's work toward recapturing one's humanity, kindness, and caring about oneself and the world of others. One gets closer to whom one is in their depth, toward one's ability to care about oneself and others. Quoting Heidegger, he states that *care* is how we identify with our humanity:

> Care, as a primordial structural totality, lies 'before' every factical 'attitude' and 'situation'" of [humans], and it does so existentially *a priori*; this means that it always lies *in* them" (Heidegger, 1962, pp. 238-239).

Heidegger discusses how one eventually reflects upon one's humanity through *care*. One's humanity is supported by one's understanding and ability to care, and this *caring side* of the personality existed even before consciousness emerged.

Working with paranoid clients can prove as challenging as any other psychological issue, and it may take some time to understand and recognize paranoia in our clients. I like to liken therapy to a pot of soup; we see how the many ingredients (constituents) blend, probably cooking for many years in the unconscious, forming complex and distorted ways of thinking and feeling about the world. One's paranoid beliefs are their own, but from the healthy-minded individual's view, there are no spies out there ready to pounce, no unknown-other who watches and talks from a distance. It is oneself who has turned against oneself, turned suspicious, frightened, demanding, and controlling. Like this soupy mixture, the therapist and client, together, remove one ingredient at a time, inspect it, taste it, talk about it thoroughly, but they must put it back because it is integral to their current life, as it has been integrated into their paranoid personality for many years.

As therapists, we do not have the right to take anything away from our clients. We cannot insist that they see things our way; we let them do the personal elimination if they are emotionally strong enough and capable of doing so. As we examine the constituents of this paranoia-soup over and over again, the ingredients may lose their strength, appeal, and ability to dominate the rest of the soup. It is with this repeated process of examination of the various and intermixed ingredients we hope paranoia loses its power over the individual's personality.

By understanding and therapeutically analyzing one's life—especially trust issues, loneliness, and pseudo self-esteem—one may reduce paranoia's domination and control over life, decrease one's thoughts and beliefs previously seen only through the paranoid lens, and integrate a more healthy lifestyle and belief system in one's personality. One's life-soup becomes more palatable and digestible. One may then welcome the opportunity to share it with others. Therapy can help a person deal with paranoia. It can help them make very important changes to how they live, think, and feel about themself and others.

As is common with everyone who has problems—physical, medical, psychological, or relationship—everyone has a story to tell. This story is quite pronounced at the beginning of one's therapy. The paranoid person has a story they *need* to tell. They may not trust the therapist, but for whatever reason they have ended up in the analysand chair, there will be a forthcoming story about their life. It is very important for the client to tell their story and to be heard. It helps with building trust and rapport. It helps the therapist know where this person has been, how they got to be where they are today, and to know them as this person with their thoughts, feelings, and beliefs.

But after a while, the therapist does not need to hear the story again once it has been told. We expect the paranoid client to discuss how they became paranoid, as described in their story. The client needs to talk about their underlying problems: anger, fear, depression, anxiety, memories, loneliness, distrust, etc. These are the problems supporting the story just told. The correct "direction" in therapy then is to move deeper into those problems—self-identity, distrust, fears, anxiety, loneliness, and emotional difficulties—in all their varieties and permeations.

If they insist on retelling their story, they are trying to avoid the real work of therapy. They are avoiding depth. They are avoiding change and healing. It is up to the therapist to gently redirect the client back to their problems, to focusing in-depth on the constituents of paranoia. On and on this process goes as one grows deeper into one's psyche, beyond the "I don't know," into one's depth, working at healing and recovery.

INFLUENCES OF COMPLEXES

Siegel used, as a metaphor, the description of paranoia as a demon hiding in the brain, but we know there is no actual demonic possession, no external entity living within us and controlling us. I make this point because some paranoid people believe they are "possessed" by something from outside of them when instead, they are under the control of an unconscious paranoia complex.

Complexes are dominated by an archetypal influence, as described previously. Once we find that influence, we have a greater chance of finding the early influences that set paranoia on its course, and helping our client work on those underlying

243

influences and all the related emotions that have been avoided and repressed. Paranoia is not a possession from the "outside" but a way of avoiding the development of our true self—who we are and have the potential to become.

INDIVIDUATION AND GUILT

This paranoid-living-in-the-world does not exist "inside" our brain but in our way of being, our beliefs, our fears, and our avoidance and neglect of becoming the individual that we can be. Therefore, I have discussed the individuation process, which is a return to ourselves and our ability to show care and honesty towards ourselves and others. While one is in therapy, one *is* walking one's path of individuation, working through emotional struggles, distrust issues, loneliness, and limiting negative feelings of self-worth. One does not emerge from therapy in a state of "perfection," but one strives to arrive at Oneself. Does this "Oneself" include paranoia tendencies? Maybe, but paranoia need not be the main content or sustained focus of one's life anymore.

We have interests and plans for our life that only we can achieve. Do we decide what abilities we pursue, or are we pre-determined to follow a path created by other people or by God? To whom do we owe our identity and determination? We have a conscious path to live and are responsible for working toward our goals. What happens if we do not achieve our goals? Whom do we blame? Are we guilty if we do not achieve self-actualization?

This is *existential* guilt. It informs us that we must achieve our life goals, and if we slack off and ignore ourselves, we *are* guilty of not succeeding. Existential guilt lives with us as we move through life. If our decisions push us towards becoming ourselves, we continue to feel activated. If our decisions work against our success, we are indeed guilty. This guilt feels like depression, anxiety, defeat, uncaringness towards others, restriction, and limitation.

Self-actualization is not a want, but a need—our own exclusive path we expect ourselves to travel. If we get sidetracked and aren't confronting and moving beyond our anxiety and limitations, how will we ever become the individual we are? Who were we before the birth of our ego, when consciousness forced the development of our individuation path upon us?

DEFINITION OF PARANOIA

This is how I would now define paranoia. I believe it to be an accurate description of how paranoia lives in the lives of paranoid individuals, and so a more concise definition of paranoia can now be written:

> Paranoia is the angry, fearful, and suspicious lifestyle of the chronically lonely, distrustful, and low-esteemed individual. Paranoid individuals, in order to avoid responsibility for their own inadequate self-esteem, believe they must protect themselves from others witnessing them as such.

I do not know if one can ever shed their paranoia completely. The National Institute of Mental Health says "no," and no other literature substantiates the ability of one to overcome paranoia completely. But what I have found is that the paranoid foundation can slowly dissolve. One may continue being suspicious but without the fear and anger associated with unresolved inner conflicts. One may learn to trust and improve authentic self-esteem. One can follow one's inner path toward self-actualization and continue finding one's authentic way through life,

but *we* must do it. Rollo May gives us something very important to think about:

> Indeed, the whole existential approach is
> rooted in the always curious phenomenon
> that we have in man a being who not only
> *can* but *must*, if he is to realize himself, ques-
> tion his own being. ...The capacity to tran-
> scend the situation is an inseparable part
> of self-awareness, for it is obvious that the
> mere awareness of oneself as a being in the
> world implies the capacity to stand outside
> and look at oneself and the situation and to
> assess and guide oneself by an infinite vari-
> ety of possibilities (May, 1983, p. 147).

The foundation of solid trust in relationships goes a long
way toward supporting a strong emotional base from which
paranoid people can find the strength to deal with all aspects of
their life among others.

This has been a study of paranoia. Does it hold weight?
Does it reveal how the essence of paranoia can be understood?
Van den Berg had a much better way of stating the point I'm
trying to question when he says:

> The reader has a right to use his own mind
> upon finishing this book, even if the sub-
> ject is outside his own area of competence;
> for the reader also shares the same human
> existence that makes this study, if I may be
> permitted to say so, also concern his life
> (van den Berg, 1972, p. 4).

We can recognize paranoia because it is a common phenomenon and study it because we are intelligent beings. We

may not all be paranoid, but we could benefit from understanding paranoia in its basic structure. I hope the depth of this book helps clarify the essence of paranoia and assists you when working with your own paranoia, if indeed you are paranoid, and with the paranoid client.

THANK YOU FOR READING

The Voice of Paranoia!

I hope the concepts and research found in my book have given you further insight and understanding of the paranoid individual. If you enjoyed this book, I would love to hear about it in a review. I welcome your feedback.

Thank You!

Let's Connect

Email: <u>dmink.lpc@gmail.com</u>

To keep up on the latest news and any upcoming books, I hope you'll connect with me today. I look forward to hearing from you.

All the best,
Daniel

ABOUT THE AUTHOR

D ANIEL HAS BEEN A LICENSED
Professional Counselor in the
State of West Virginia for the past
25 years. He has worked as a psychotherapist in private practice for most
of those years, concerning himself
with all mental illnesses and mental
health states. He worked at Shuman
Detention Center in Pittsburgh on
the locked jail ward for teenage violent sex offenders, and on
the locked units of the county psychiatric hospital in Beckley,
WV. He has been interested in understanding paranoia since
his childhood, wondering why he was so afraid and distrustful
of others, and why he felt he was the center of others' negative
attention.

Daniel got his undergraduate degree in mathematics and
computer science, working for twelve years in banking and
insurance. One day he finally said, "Enough; I find no meaning in working with computers anymore." It was then that
he quit computer work and went to graduate school studying Existential-Phenomenological psychology at Duquesne
University, a school specializing in the humanistic approach to
understanding human nature. Daniel became a member of the
C. G. Jung Educational Center in Pittsburgh, PA, for ten years,
stating, "Jung makes psychology come alive." Upon moving to
West Virginia, Daniel taught psychology at the local commu-

nity college as an adjunct instructor for fourteen years and is currently an active member of the WV Licensed Professional Counselors Association.

Daniel has many interests and hobbies, including gardening, karate, woodworking, and reading. He lives in Beckley, WV, with his wife, Debi, and several dogs, cats, and chickens. He enjoys swimming and playing with his five grandchildren.

BIBLIOGRAPHY

Association, A. P. (2013).*Diagnostic and Statistical Manual on Mental Disorders* (5th ed.). American Psychiatric Publishing.

Baumeister, R. F., Campbell, J. D., Krueger, J. I., & Vohs, K. D. (2005). Exploding The Self-Esteem Myth. *Scientific Amercian Mind , 16* (4).

Branden, N. (1994). *The Six Pillars of Self-Esteem.* New York: Bantam.

Branden, N. (1994). *The Six Pillars of Self-Esteem.* New York: Bantam.

Brown, J. D., & Marshall, M. A. (2006). *The Three Faces of Self-Esteem. In M. Kernis (Ed.), Self-esteem: Issues and answers (pp.4-9).* New York: Psychology Press.

Cacioppo, J. T., Cacioppo, S., Cole, S. W., Capitanio, J. P., Goossens, L., & Boomsma, D. I. (2015). Loneliness Across Phylogeny and a Call for Comparative Studies and Animal Models. *Perspective on Psychological Science , ?,*02-212.

DeBecker, G. (1997). *The Gift of Fear.* New York: Dell Publishing.

Edinger, E. F. (1995). *The Mysterium Lectures.* Toronto: Inner City Books.

Erikson, E. H. (1950/1963). *Childhood and Society* (2nd Edition ed.). New York: W. W. Norton & Company, Inc.

Erikson, E. H. (1968). *Identity - Youth and Crisis.* New York: W. W. Norton & Compane, Inc.

Fisher, W. F. (1988). *Theories of Anxiety* (2nd ed.). Lanham, MD: University Press of America, Inc.

Freeman, D. G. (2005). Psychologial investigation of the structure of paranoia in the non-clinical population. *The British Journal of Psychiatry* , 186:427-435.

Freud, S. (1911, 2003). *The Schreber Case.* (A. Webber, Trans.) New York: Penguin Books.

Fuller, A. R. (1990). *Insight Into Value.* Albany: State University of New York Press.

Hawley, K. (2012). *Trust - A Very Short Introduction.* Oxford, U.K.: Oxford University Press.

Heidegger, M. (1962). *Being and Time.* (J. Macquarrie, & E. Robinson, Trans.) New York: Harper & Row.

Jung, C. G. (1971). *Psychological Types.* (R. F. Hull, Trans.) Princeton, NJ: Princeton University Press.

Jung, C. G. (1959). *The Archetypes and the Collective Unconscious* (2nd ed., Vol. 9. Part I. Bollingen Series XX). (R. F. Hull, Trans.) Princeton University Press.

Jung, C. G. (1954). *The Development of Personality* (Vol. 17). (H. Read, M. Fordham, G. Adler, W. McGuire, Eds., & R. F. Hull, Trans.) New York: Princeton University Press.

Jung, C. G. (1954/1966). *The Practice of Psychotherapy* (2nd Edition ed.). (R. F. Hull, Trans.) Princeton, N. J.: Princeton University Press.

Jung, C. G. (1960). *The Psychogenesis of Mental Disease* (Vol. 3). (R. F. Hull, Trans.) Princeton, NJ: Princeton University Press.

Jung, C. G. (1969). *The Structure and Dynamics of the Psyche* (2nd ed.). (R. F. Hull, Trans.) Princeton, N.J.: Princeton University Press.

Jung, C. G. (1953). *Two Essays on Analytical Psychology.* (R. F. Hull, Trans.) NY: Princeton University Press.

Kantor, M. (2004). *Understanding Paranoia.* Westport, CN: Praeger Publishers.

Kapleau, P. (1980). *The Three Pillars of Zen.* New York: Anchor Books.

Knowles, R. T. (1986). *Human Development and Human Possibility.* Lanham, Maryland: University Press of America.

Laing, R. D. (1961). *Self and Others.* New York: Pantheon Books.

Maslow, A. H. (1943/2013). *A Theory of Human Motivation.* Mancsfield Centre: Martino Publishing.

May, R. (1983). *The Discovery of Being.* New York: W. W. Norton & Company.

Meissner, W. W. (1986). *Psychotherapy and the Paranoid Process.* Norvale, NJ: Jason Aronson, Inc.

Merleau-Ponty, M. (1964). *The Primacy of Perception.* (J. Wild, Ed.) Northwestern University Press.

Miller, A. (1983). *For Your Own Good.* (H. Hunter, & H. Hunter, Trans.) New York: Farrar, Strau, Giroux.

Moustakas, C. E. (1961). *Loneliness.* New York: Prentice Hall Press.

Muuss, R. E. (1996). *Theories of Adolescence* (6th ed.). (B. Kaufman, & F. H. Burns, Eds.) New York: McGraw-Hill.

Neumann, E. (1954). *The Origin and History of Consciousness.* (R. F. Hull, Trans.) Princeton: Princeton University Press.

Reps, P. (1935). *Zen Flesh, Zen Bones.* New York: Anchor Books.

Rogers, C. R. (1961). *On Becoming A Person.* Boston: Houghton Mifflin Company.

Saint John, o. t. (1991). *The collected Works of St. John of the Cross.* (K. Kavanaugh, & O. Rodriguez, Trans.) Washington, DC: Institute of Carmelite Studies Publications.

Shalit, E. (2002). *The Complex: Path of Transformation from Archetype to Ego.* Toronto: Inner City Books.

Shapiro, D. (1981). *Autonomy and Rigid Character.* Basic Books.

Siegel, R. K. (1994). *Whispers The voice of Paranoia.* New York: Simon & Schuster Paperbacks.

Sullivan, H. S. (1953). *The Interpersonal Theory of Psychiatry.* New York: W. W. Norton & Company.

The Free Dictionary. (2019). Retrieved November 20, 2019, from The Free Dictionary, Medical-Dictionary: http://medical-dictionary.thefreedictionary.com

Tillich, P. (1952, 2000). *The Courage To Be* (2nd ed.). Yale University Press.

van den Berg, J. H. (1972). *A Different Existence.* Pittsburgh: Duquesne University Press.

Van Epp, J. (2007). *How to Avoid Falling in Love with a Jerk.* New York: McGraw-Hill.

van Kaam, A. (1969). *Existential Foundations of Psychology.* New York: Image Books.

Yalom, I. D. (1980). *Existential Psychotherapy.* Basic Books.

Young-Eisendrath, P. (2008). *The Self-esteem Trap.* New York: Little, Brown and Company.

INDEX

255